hello

Budweiser
UFILTRERET
DANSK PILSNER
ROYAL EXPORT
ROYAL PILSNER
Lærke
LÆNGE LEVE
ØL

Handknit designer anno 2023
SECURITY

Netflix
WeTransfer - Send Large Files &
IMG_1343.JPG
Åbn med Billedfremviser

babe

Lærke Bagger

Knit it out

PRESTEL
Munich · London · New York

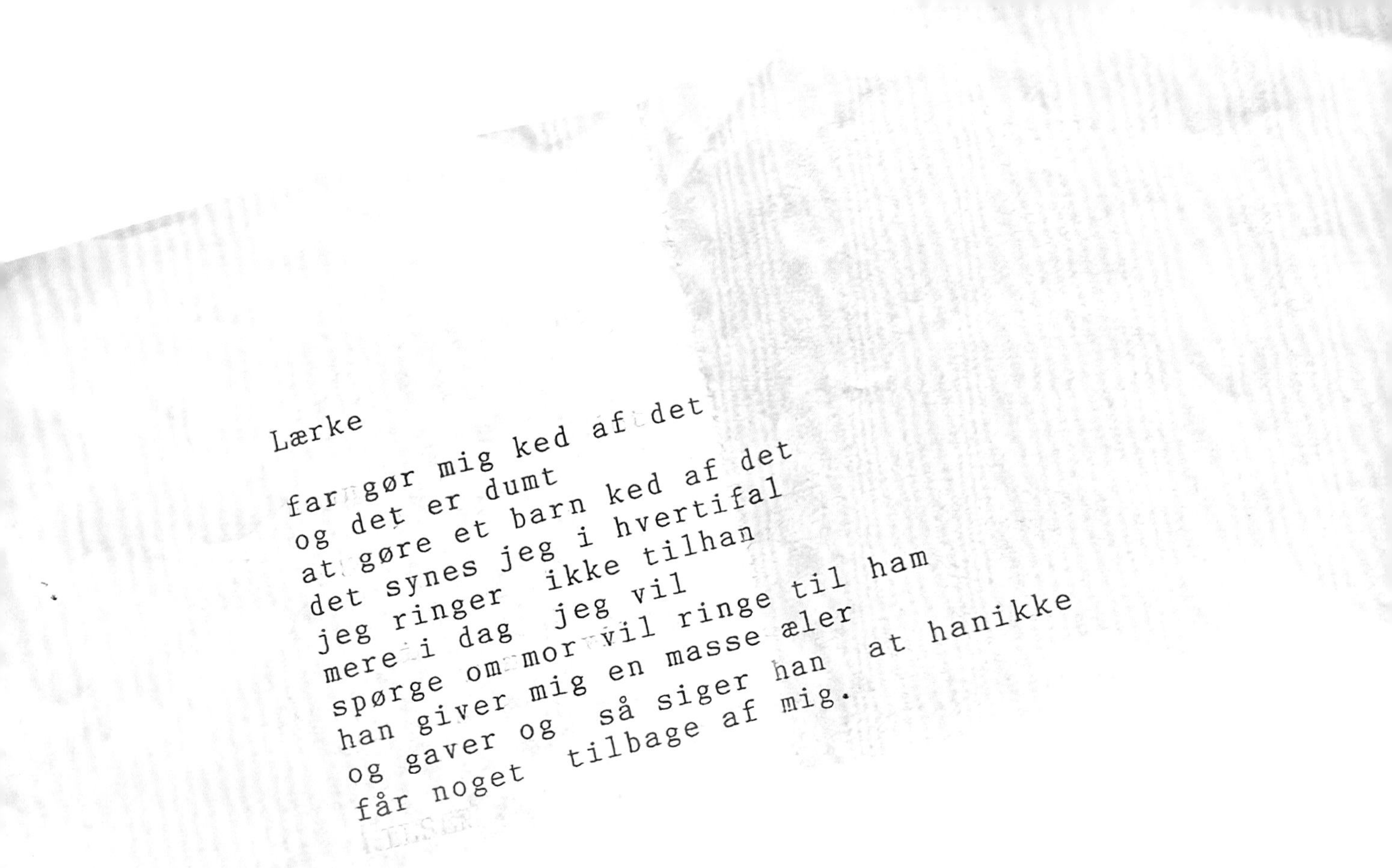

Lærke

far gør mig ked af det
og det er dumt
at gøre et barn ked af det
det synes jeg i hvertifal
jeg ringer ikke tilhan
mere i dag jeg vil
spørge om mor vil ringe til ham
han giver mig en masse æler
og gaver og så siger han at hanikke
får noget tilbage af mig.

Cover: Luisa Klose on the basis of a design by Spine Studio and
using graphic elements by Nadiinko / stock.adobe.com and
Ditte Vejlstrup / tlm0n344 / stock.adobe.com

First published in Danish under the title *Laerke Bagger. Strik 2*
by Gyldendal Nonfiktion, Klareboderne 3, 1115 Copenhagen

Published by agreement with Gyldendal Group Agency

For the English Edition

A member of Penguin Random House Verlagsgruppe GmbH
Neumarkter Strasse 28 · 81673 Munich

Library of Congress Control Number is available; a CIP catalogue record for this book
is available from the British Library.

Illustrationen: Ditte Vejlstrup / t1m0n344 / stock.tock.adobe.com
Photos by Laerke Bagger, Sidsel Alling, Henning Bagger and Sune Christiansen
Design and layout: Spine Studio

Editorial direction Prestel: Andrea Bartelt-Gering
Translation from German: Melanie Girdlestone
Copyediting: Barbara Holland
Coordination: booklab GmbH, Munich
Production management: Luisa Klose
Satz: Rüdiger Wagner, BUCHFLINK
Printing and binding: ROTOLITO S.p.A., Milano

MIX
Paper | Supporting responsible forestry
FSC® C005461

Penguin Random House Verlagsgruppe FSC® N001967

Printed in Italy
ISBN 978-3-7913-8045-2
www.prestel.com

Lærke

Dad upset me. It's so stupid to upset a kid. At least, that's what I think. I'm not going to call him any more today. I'll ask Mum to call him. He keeps giving me stuff and then saying he never gets anything back.

If you can't be a rockstar, you can at least be a knitwear designer...

IMG_1154.JPG
Åbn med Billedfremviser

okay

Chapter 4

Chapter 5

Chapter 6

27 December 2021

Dear Dad,

All I ever wanted was to have contact with you, for us to be close, and for me to know I'm exactly the daughter you wanted. Because that way I wouldn't have to prove anything or be someone I'm not. I could just be who I am. Good or bad.

The reality is, you probably never gave yourself the opportunity to meet me. Maybe you were scared to find out who I am? Or scared that I might be something you don't understand or that you feel you can't live up to. Maybe parents are more scared of their kids not accepting them than the other way round? Maybe us parents know we'll never be good enough, no matter how hard we try?

I've just started writing the first few pages of this book, which is going to be about us two. It's been a terrible morning. Not one of my finest moments as a parent. I did what you did: all the things I never wanted to do. I'm now sitting at my computer crying, just like I used to when I read your long emails about all my failings as a daughter. Beside me is the mug I bought you, which I had intended to give you for Christmas. It says "Merry Christmas Grandad" and has a photo of Lulu on it, age one, sitting in the bath. The mug never reached you. Ten days after I ordered it, you died. But in actual fact, the mug is lying anyway. You weren't a grandad. Henning is one, and he's earned his right to the title.

But hey, that's not what this is about. I didn't want to upset you just before you died. Maybe that's been our problem all our lives: we never say the whole truth, just fragments of it, embroidered with the occasional white lie here and there.

On the table is my knitting, for #nofearkal, a knitting community about facing up to your fears and doing stuff anyway. As I write, I'm full of worries. I'm worried about writing this book. I worry about going through losing you again. I'm worried everyone might find out I'm as rubbish as you said I was. And I'm worried I might realise how rubbish I am myself.

Prologue

Knitting is the spark within you. I’m here to ignite it – and to keep the flame alive.

Within me, there's a spark. The moment it ignites, the fire spreads and spreads, I notice. Whenever I feel I have to pretend I'm an author, the first thing I do is get my own fire going so I can really start writing this book, which is about the most difficult subject in my life: my relationship with my father. It was difficult and full of anger. My father is half of me, and yet he's not really half of me at all. He lives in me, though. I don't feel I know or understand him or our relationship. Not yet. But this book is my attempt to tackle my grief through knitting.

This book is my difficult second book. The patterns, techniques and texts in my new book are a bit more challenging than in my first one, and as life gets harder for me, so it gets harder for my readers too. In fact, everything about this book is a bit more challenging. Including the emotions. But then, who cares about easy stuff anyway? Easy is boring. It's as boring as it is perfect, whereas challenges help us grow. In knitting and in life. While I was working on this book, I grew to love nature. I've always been quite sceptical about nature, but it's amazing how you can keep on learning all your life.

A few years ago my dad died. He used to walk down the street looking like a goddam rockstar. But he didn't give a sh*t about it. He had this really cool walk, almost with a bit of a dance in his step. I was proud to walk beside him, and my mother often said, "You walk just like Jørn." Every time she says it, I feel happy and sad at the same time. Happy because I have inherited something from him that only us two have, and sad because I am starting to forget the way he walked. I'm also sad because it seems I don't take after him all that much really. Do I really just walk like him? Surely there's more than that?

Actually, my father and I never really had the opportunity to find out how similar we were – or not. For a long time, I had this recurring dream that he was listening to me telling him who I am, so he could get to know me. Dear dad, I know that, if you had got to know me, you would've been proud of me.

This book is for everyone who has felt wrong at some time. Or who still feels wrong. Because if you just let that feeling happen, there's a lot you can gain. My dream is for you to knit every single item in this book as though it was your last pullover on this earth, for you to give it your all, to give everything, to really throw yourself into it. My new book is for beginners and advanced knitters. It contains 12 knitting patterns with more than 30 variations. In it, I also explain how you can re-interpret the knitting patterns in infinite different ways, depending on your mood, personality, materials, and life situation.

The mantra of this book is: Knit it out. And, believe me, I know a lot about how knitting can save your mind. When I'm really, really sad, all I want to do is knit. It's the same when I'm feeling stressed. Amid all the uncertainty, handicrafts have always been my safe haven. They are the place I go to for refuge.

When you're someone's child, you stay their child forever. This book is maybe my – perhaps rather childish – attempt to get to know a father that I never really knew. My father loved books and probably had about 40 boxes of them when he died. Maybe he would've liked the fact that I am a writer?

In this book I tell the story of myself and my father as well as I possibly can. Every design in this book is built on important memories, on stories told through my knitting needles, stitches and yarn. Sometimes I really can't find the words to capture every detail, so in a way, this is a biography in knitting. Maybe you have a story to tell too, through your own knitted biography, through pullovers, scarves, dresses, coats and cushions.

My collection of knitting stuff is always a random assortment of yarns that tell the story of a life full of love, joy, misunderstandings, shame, and lots and lots of anger. Luckily, though, knitting is very forgiving, and no matter how good or beautiful you are, with your needles and yarn you can always be happy, or escape, or think things through. Your knitting is yours, and it's done your way. Sometimes it's fine not to go all the way – it's the same in my life: I've got heaps of unfinished knitting projects and experiences waiting for me.

I love clothes. My father thought they were ridiculous – which I took to mean that I was ridiculous. But knitting is my pathway through life. So, let's follow our pathway together! Even when life is tough and hurts, even when we feel wrong. Nobody will be left on their own, whether as a knitting designer on a podium or at the cemetery, next to her dead father, who she never really knew.

Knit it out.

Best,
Lærke

hello

1985
Born in Aalborg.

1993
Started knitting.

2008
Internship with the knitwear designer Isabel Berglund.

2009
Started at the Royal Danish Academy of Fine Arts, School of Design, Copenhagen.

2013
Internship with the fashion label Sibling, London.

2015
Masters in Design at the Royal Danish Academy of Fine Arts.

2017
Creative Director for Hjertegarn.

2020
Reached 100,000 followers on Instagram; nominated Newcomer Of The Year in the Elle Style Awards.

2021
Debut as a writer.

· packshots
- never gin
- Diddl
- stickers
- diagrammer
• hår mascara

babygirl
HOUSE MUSIC

Chapter 1

The apple orchard, my first time knitting, and why Barbie is so much more than just a toy.

When I was a kid, I fell over and broke a tooth. So I have a dark tooth in all the photos. In this one, my hair had just been cut short, by the way!

My story is nothing special. It might be quite banal. But it's mine. And it's a classic. Someone has a child. That child is me. For various reasons, the someone finds it hard being a grown-up parent. So the child takes responsibility and feels guilty. The child and parent have a complex lifelong on-off relationship. The parent gets old and dies (far too young). By this time, the child is grown up and misses, loves and grieves for her parent – and feels more and more guilty; she blames herself more and more.

In 1993 I was eight years old. My father was a nurse and had an apple orchard. He loved nature, and he loved to help people. Especially if they didn't have anyone else. So, when I was little, I would often be left, sitting on a park bench with these men and women – and all their bottles – while my father went to the kiosk to buy beer and cigarettes. Not for himself but for them. That's what he was like when he had money. He liked to give it away. He certainly wasn't mean.

My father always wore jeans, an open shirt and a T-shirt with a thick, rugged, knitted pullover that was already quite elderly. The kind of pullover, in other words, that was passed down the generations and that's made of such good wool that it's almost too hot to wear. They were a bit scratchy too, those pullovers. He looked more like a rock'n'roller than a nurse or an apple farmer, and he had the biggest LP collection I've ever seen. He had thick, curly hair and tinted aviator glasses. Actually, I quite often dress the same way, only without the warm pullover, but a lot of days I really do wear a lumberjack shirt and tee. Maybe because it helps me feel close to him. Or because we both like checks and soft cotton. Who knows?

I used to spend every other weekend at my dad's, in his orchard. The rest of the time I lived with my mother, in the city, where I had lots of Barbie dolls, smart clothes, glittery colours, and so on. But at his house I had knives, overalls and trees for climbing in. I even had my own little axe and was actually pretty good at splitting firewood. I don't think my mother knew I was splitting firewood when I was eight. My father never actually said it was a secret, but I somehow could sense it was. We had quite a lot of non-secrets like that, my dad and me. Like the time I sat on the cargo deck of his pickup all the way from Aalborg to Støvring; or the time I rode all the way home from kindergarten on the front of his motorbike with him – without a helmet; or the time he cut my hair short without asking my mum first. I think he would have liked me to have been a boy. Maybe just because it would have been easier with a boy. At least, that's what it felt like by the time I was eight.

The orchard was near Rold Skov, a stunningly beautiful place in northern Jutland. My dad would pick the mouldy brown apples up off the ground, put his head right back and squeeze the juice out, letting it drop into his mouth. Then he would help me do the same. When he did that, I thought he was the coolest dad in the world. The juice tasted divine, but with all that mould going on, it was enough to get totally plastered! The apples had fermented!

I was allowed to run around all over the place in the orchard and the adjacent forest, but not in the barn where the apple presses were. Most of the time I had just my dad's dog for company. My dad gave me a little red boiler suit that I wore most of the time, while he wore a blue one.

As a kid, I was two different people, trying to make everybody's life simpler and my father happy. I was one child at my dad's house and a different one at my mum's. I really wanted to make my dad proud of me, so I did my best to be the kind of kid that would fit into his life: a Thing-Finder that carves sticks, collects stones and is outdoors from morning to night – and loving it. But the truth is, I didn't. When I was a kid, the things I loved most of all were playing with my Barbies, drawing clothes, embroidering floor cushions and watching TV. The same things I still love today.

I really remember missing him. I missed him every day and found myself longing for something that actually never existed. As a child, yearning, missing and hope were my faith. I also remember just as vividly the disappointments, the awkwardness of it all and feeling homesick. I just wanted to get back to the city, to my mum, to security and my Barbies.

I never felt secure at my dad's place because I never knew what was going to happen. I tried to be the kid he wanted but ended up feeling lonely and inadequate because I never managed. After all, I was just me, nobody else. I also remember distinctly the massive sense of relief I felt on Sunday evenings when I got back home to my mum's and my Barbies. Finally, I could breathe normally again and just be myself.

I loved my Barbies (confession: I still love Barbies today). When I was little, I would spend hours creating outfits for them, for different occasions: Barbie at work, Barbie at a party, Barbie on a beach holiday, Barbie at the supermarket. Outfits, outfits, outfits. I don't remember ever playacting stuff like Hello-my-name's-Barbie with my dolls; all I ever did was combine and create clothes.

My father thought the Barbie world was really silly and that clothes existed for just one practical reason: to keep people warm and protect them from the cold and rain. My father thought concentrating on your appearance was a sign of a weak character. To him, looks were irrelevant, a waste of time, totally demeaning, even, and a sign of weakness. He told me that often enough.

My handicrafts belonged to me alone,
a place of freedom, where nobody could get too close
or bully me. I had the whole world in my hands,
waiting for me to conquer it, stitch by stitch.
Nothing was impossible. And nor is it now.

But to me, clothes are about so much more than practicality. Clothes are an extension of your personality. They are a form of expression that tells stories about our time, origins and values. They can also make you feel secure. They can show where you belong, but also provoke people. Clothes can lift your mood or suppress it, look attractive or repulsive. I have always loved combining different styles, epochs and silhouettes, and I love mixing the feminine with the masculine. I love getting all dressed up for no reason, being beautiful and sexy, showing off and filling the room. But I also like understatement, hiding, relaxing, letting go and watching instead of being watched. I am very proud of my relationship with clothes. Now.

It was actually the same with my Barbies when I was little. But I was too young to express myself through my clothes, let alone make my own stuff to wear. Instead, I did Barbie fashion shows and designed collections. Creativity and making things were all that mattered. As soon as I had designed something and styled my Barbies, the fun bit was over. Which is almost exactly the way I earn a crust today.

Sadly, my father didn't get it. Every year I wanted a new Barbie for my birthday or Christmas, and every year he would give me a new knife or toolbox. I once got a stuffed rabbit – a real one – which upset me no end. I wept over the "dead baby bunny" for hours.

I recently bought myself two Barbies I've always wanted. (I know! I'm a grown-up! But I just had to have these two Benetton Barbies!) They are from 1990 – when I was five – and they are still in their boxes. I would love to unpack them and play with them. One day, maybe. But they look so beautiful in their boxes. I'll probably buy a few more.

There's no getting away from yourself in life. That's important to remember. So, instead, be proud of yourself. Live with it. As I write the words, "I love watching telly. I love clothes, I love Barbies, and I love myself for loving those things", I am saying them out loud.

I first started knitting when I was eight. Even now I distinctly remember how it felt to hold something I had made myself in my hands, that was created by me and me alone, and where I had made all the decisions. There were no strings attached and no expectations to meet. Just a bit of wool that was nothing until I made it into something. My handicrafts belonged to me alone. They were a place of freedom, where nobody could get too close or bully me. I had the whole world in my hands, waiting for me to conquer it, stitch by stitch. Nothing was impossible. And nor is it now.

Oh, how I loved Barbies! And I still do today, in fact!

Barbie
Barbie

Barbie

1994

FARMOR

You're not doing anything wrong, and there are no wrong colours or yarns. (*3-Day Sweater/Dress/Top/Skirt*, page 54).

The Inner Child technique

Let's start with a real challenge: forget all the boring, sensible, grown-up ways of doing things that you have learned. Just let them go. That's exactly what I do. I'd like to see my eight-year-old self and tell her everything will be fine and that, for God's sake, it's not your fault, it's your dad's! It's him that's the grown-up! I would also tell myself that just because I'm not the kid he wanted, it doesn't mean I'm wrong. And I'd say: "In 30 years' time, all these difficult feelings and experiences will enable you to create totally insane clothes. And believe me: you'll be going a hundred miles an hour, no matter what people say. Because people *will* say things. A lot!"

What I'd like to say to you is exactly what I would say to my younger self: "You are right. Nobody is wrong. And you have to try and be 100 percent yourself, even if it's hard."

By knitting, I am probably trying to regain a bit of my childhood. I mean – dammit! – let's all get our childhoods back! Let's remember, recognise, work through, try to understand, celebrate and create – without fear or embarrassment. Together! This is where we rediscover our goddam inner child, because there's a great big world out there, and the most important thing you have is your curiosity.

Knit yourself free and let your knitting be what it is. No more, no less. It won't disappoint you, I promise. You can do (pretty much) anything, and the worst that can happen is you'll scrape a knee because you ran too fast or jumped too high. Close your eyes and feel the sense that anything is possible. Be curious about what, how and why. If your knitting is going to look crap, accept it. Who cares? Because the whole point of *Inner Child* is something quite different: it's about cleansing, creating space, giving yourself air to breathe, getting things in order, liberating yourself, stimulation and moving forward.

HJERTEGARN A/S
Since 1926

How to knit with the Inner Child technique

From your stash of yarns, choose a few you like and that you're curious to try out, that you don't understand, perhaps, or feel drawn to. Get a sense of yourself, how you feel, the kind of mood you're in. Don't think about what you can and can't do in terms of materials, colours, tension and stuff like that. Forget stuff you can't do anything about – because that kind of stuff is toxic. *Inner Child* is about being free to do absolutely anything. Pick out 5 or even 40 different yarns, just on impulse, yarns you feel drawn to, that speak to you.

Now go crazy. Forget what they taught you at school, and what your mum, grandma and great-grandma (or whoever taught you to knit) told you and just cut, tie, knot and make holes as though there's no tomorrow. Practise acting on impulse. 100%. Just do what you want, when you want, even if the (sensible) grown-up in you is telling you you're doing it all wrong. If you find you can't let go, set yourself some rules and make sure you follow them. Things like, "After 25 stitches, cut the yarn and do the next bit with a really hideous colour." It's a lot more fun than it sounds, I swear!

The ribbing is your safety net. It sets the framework for your design and gives you a safe space and the security to give up control completely. For your ribbing, choose a basic yarn (p. 234) and a main colour you like, one that goes well with something you already have in your wardrobe or that you find calming, perhaps. Basically, a yarn you feel good about. Personally, I like no-bullsh*t yarns, the kind of stuff you can knit on size 5 needles. That's what I recommend for the *Inner Child Sweater* on page 48. (For more on the different yarn types, see p. 254.) Then, besides the yarns you have selected, choose two more basic yarns in other colours to give yourself a break from time to time. Preferably colours that make you feel safe and happy.

If you're doing *Inner Child*, personally, I don't think you need to do a tension square. Just let your pullover, dress, crop top or whatever be your tension square instead. Or knit a little Barbie sweater (p. 52). Experiment a bit. You might end up with a great work of art – or a great lesson in what never to do again. Either is good. And that's also why I'm not a fan of unravelling things – because we are the sum of our mistakes and experiences. They make us what we are. And we should be proud of them all.

If you have trouble getting started, close your eyes and think back to when you were a child. To a happy memory, perhaps, or a sad one. Where were you? What were you wearing? What did it smell like in that place? How did you feel? What colours and objects do you remember? Now try and knit those memories with your yarns and materials.

Knit holes (p. 43) wherever you feel like it. Knit lots of them, just a few, or maybe even a whole row. Personally, I like holes to be random and impulsive, but I also like to add a few when I'm knitting stripes and changing between two colours, for instance.

Switch between all different types of yarn and colours. Thick, thin, smooth, fluffy. Switch at the beginning, middle or end of a row or round. Who cares? Just as long as you keep switching. I love print and special-effect yarns (p. 212) for *Inner Child*, because I think they make a nice addition to the look. Use black, white, beige or grey when you need

When you're doing *Inner Child*, use old photos of yourself as a child for inspiration, or just go with your colours, materials, patterns and mood.

a break, to calm things down a bit. (By the way, there's a mini-guide to selecting and switching colours on p. 237.)

Before you start knitting, you might like to sketch your pullover. Or get your kids, grandkids or some other kiddie-minded person to sketch it. Maybe you can sketch it together. It could be fun. But I can't promise. After all, kids are so wonderfully direct and free from preconceived ideas. That I do know!

If you have had a bad day or feel angry with life, your boyfriend, yourself, your work, your parents or your friends, then knit it out. When life is good, knit that out too. Throw in some holes, and mix purple with black and orange. Scream at your knitting. Whisper to it. Or just enjoy it.

Oh yes, and if you're knitting thin yarn on thick needles, then whatever you do, make sure you don't knit too tight. Otherwise you won't be able to pull the stitches up and down the needle. Knit "sloppy", as my grandma used to call it. And enjoy every moment.

If you have had a bad day or feel angry with life, your boyfriend, yourself, your work, your parents or your friends, then knit it out. When life is good, knit that out too. Throw in some holes, and mix purple with black and orange. Scream at your knitting. Whisper to it. Or just enjoy it.

Seriously?!? That's just awesome, right? Btw if you'd rather make a dress than a pullover, just knit it longer. (For the *Inner Child Sweater* pattern, see p. 48.)

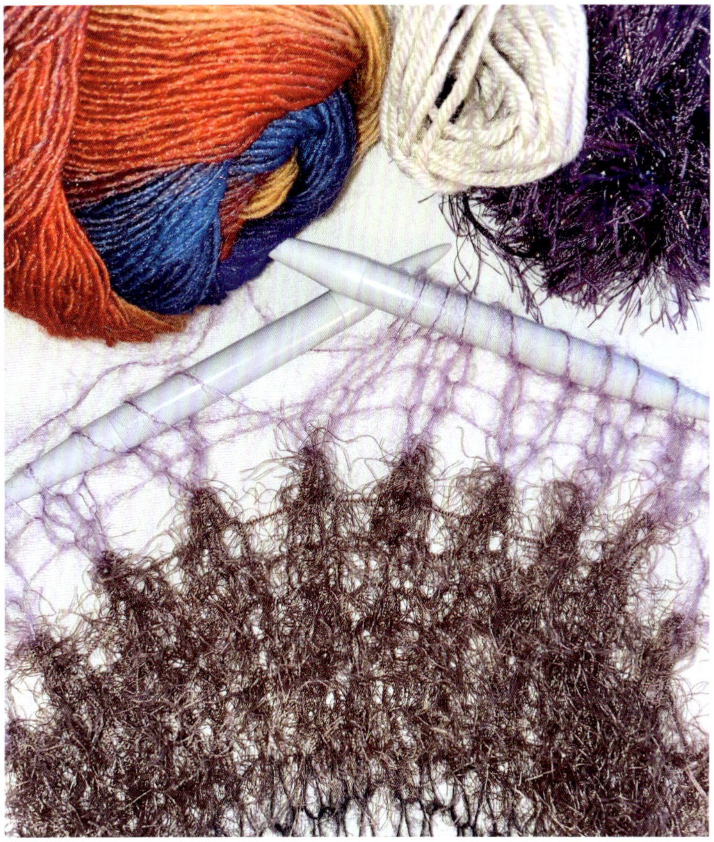

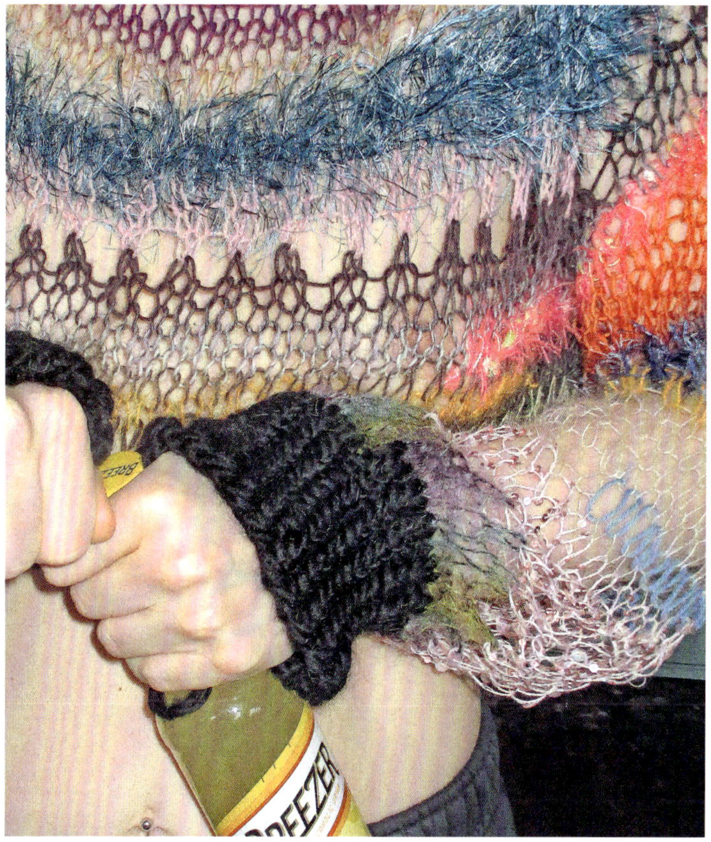

Supercool effect: a round of holes when switching colour.

Knit holes

Quite honestly, knitting holes is super-easy. Basically, you loop the yarn over the needle and then knit two together. The loop over the needle is your "new" stitch. You can also do it the other way round: knit two together and then loop the yarn over the needle. Whatever way you like.

And you can knit as many or as few holes as you want. But make sure you knit two together every time you loop the yarn over the needle, otherwise you'll end up with a different number of stitches than you started with. Then, on the row or round after you made the hole, just do purl or knit all the way (depending on whether you are doing rounds or rows, and stocking or garter stitch). Personally, I think holes look best if you knit them with the right side of your work facing you. But see what works best for you.

I love Barnaby.

Knitting a hole (in stocking or garter stitch)
Row 1 › Yarn over needle, knit 2 together (if the right side of your work is facing you).
Row 2 › Knit/purl all stitches (depending on whether you are knitting rows or rounds, and stocking or garter stitch).

Knitting a row of holes
Row 1 › *Yarn over needle, knit 2 together*. Repeat from * to * to end of row/round. You will need an even number of stitches.
Row 2 › Knit/purl all stitches (depending on whether you are knitting rows or rounds, and stocking or garter stitch)

If you have an odd number of stitches, knit the last stitch in plain. *Inner Child* is sloppy enough already. If I'm knitting a row of holes, I like to knit the first two and the last two stitches in plain because I like to have a nice edge. If I'm knitting a round of holes, I launch straight in by looping the yarn over the needle and then knitting two together, in plain.

Straps – yes or no? Plus a note on ties

Boob-tubes and bandeau tops are cute, aren't they? Oh man, the number of boob-tubes I've had! They're not just for women with small or no breasts either. They're for everyone. And you can make them with or without straps.

There are different ways of making straps, and I'm going to suggest two that everyone will love. Both involve knitting what's called an I-cord. The only difference is the way the cords are attached. If you attach them further out towards the sides of the front and back, it creates a strappy-top effect, whereas if you attach them only to the front (again, towards the sides), you have a neckholder. You can also attach the straps in the middle of the front, for a different neckholder effect.

So, what is a knitted cord anyway? Well, it's just a thin tube knitted in the round. You can either knit it straight onto your tube top or make it separately and then sew it on – for example, if you want it in the middle of the front to create a halterneck.

You can use these techniques to add a strap to any knitted piece.

How to add a strap towards the side of a front
You will need two double-pointed needles in the size specified in the knitting pattern.

Start with the left strap. Lay the top out flat in front of you. Measure 2 to 5 cm from the left-hand edge inwards, along the cast-off edge of the top. Where exactly you put the strap is entirely up to you. Some people like it to sit further out towards the edge, others prefer it a little further in, towards the middle. Now, using one of your double-pointed needles, pick up between 2 and 6 stitches along the cast-off edge by pulling the yarn through both loops of the cast-off stitches, working from left to right. (The more stitches you pick up, the wider your strap will be.) Then knit the stitches in plain. After the last stitch, don't turn the work around: instead, push the stitches to the other end of the needle and change hands. With your working needle now in your right hand, pull the yarn across the back of your work and knit the first stitch in plain. Knit every row in the same direction and in plain. The stitches will then roll up to form a tube.

Carry on knitting until your strap is 40-55 cm long, depending on how high or low you want the neck of your top. Also, if you have a larger chest, you will need longer straps. With less of a chest, shorter straps will be fine. When the strap is the right length, cut off the yarn, leaving a tail of about 10 cm, then bind off by threading the tail into a needle and pulling it clockwise through the stitches. Give it a gentle tug and pull it down behind the top few centimetres of the strap. Then give it a good tug and cut it off so that the end is hidden inside the strap. Repeat the process for the right-hand strap on the front.

You now have two straps on the front to make a nice halterneck. Job done. Alternatively, if you are making a strappy top, repeat the process on the back of your garment and create two more straps. You might like to position the back straps slightly more towards the middle than the front ones. It looks cute. You can then tie the front and back straps together on the tops of your shoulders. Awesome! You can also cross the straps so that they tie diagonally from front to back.

Centre straps (and ties)
If you want the strap in the middle of the front – for a totally different, super-cute halterneck effect – you will need to knit it separately. To do this, cast on 2-4 stitches and knit an I-cord as described above. Don't make the strap too thick, as you will need to be able to pull it through a stitch of your top later. Knit about 80-90 cm (the strap will need to be double-length, of course) and bind off as described above. Sew in the ends. Mark the middle of your top (either using a stitch counter or just by sight) and pull the strap through a hole in the ribbing. To do this, just "invent" a hole about half a centimetre below the top edge and pull the strap through. Pull the two ends to the same length. Tie them round your neck and go for it! Niiice!

You can also use this type of strap to tie a top or skirt. Depending on the look and fit of the top/skirt, roughly measure your waist, hips or chest and add about 50 cm. Then knit the strap to that length and pull it through the row of holes you knitted before casting off your top or skirt (see instructions for *3-Day Top/ Skirt*, p. 54). Tie it in a bow. For more on how to use silk or satin ribbons as ties, see page 208.

FYI › You can use these methods to make straps for any other knit that needs them.

OK, I'll admit it: I looove Barbies and tiny labels. I mean, what's not to like? The *3-Day Top or Skirt* (p. 54) looks great with a ribbon to tie it at the top, by the way.

Elasticated edges

If you knit a tube top or skirt, it's a good idea to reinforce the edges with some elastic thread (or shirring elastic), either just at the top, or at the top and bottom. Get some thin, elastic thread in a colour you think will work with your knit. It normally comes in white, black or transparent and you can get it from most craft shops. You will also need a needle with an eye that's big enough to get the elastic thread through. First of all, turn your knit inside out. You're now going to pull the elastic thread through the top row of the knitting, just below the casting-off row. That gives you the best and neatest finish.

Personally, I only pull the elastic thread through every other stitch. It's easiest if you pull it through the knit stitches of your ribbing as they are the easiest to see. So, starting on the side of your knitted piece, pull the needle with the elastic thread through the first stitch. Now, rather than knotting the thread, leave a 10 cm tail dangling – but mind it doesn't disappear into your work as you go! I've had it disappear so often and had to start over every time.

Leaving a bit hanging loose at the beginning gives you more leeway later on, when you decide how tight or loose you want the elastic to fit. Clever, huh?

Now, pull the needle and elastic thread through the stitches – but don't pull it tight just yet. We'll do that at the end. When you have worked your way round completely, cut the thread off, again leaving a 10-20 cm tail. This will allow you to adjust the stretchiness of the knitted edge as needed. Then, when you have found the tightness you want, knot the two ends of the elastic thread together, as shown on p. 237.

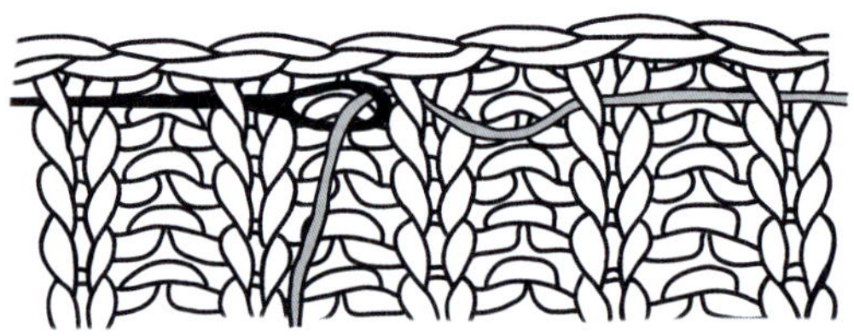

You can use this method on any garment that needs an elastic thread: for ribbing, off-the-shoulder boat necks, socks that won't stay up, etc.

A *3-Day Skirt* with *3-Day Top* (p. 54) knitted in black and multicoloured stripes with a row of holes at every colour-change. Plus a cute little scarf knitted the same way.

Instructions

Inner Child Sweater

Start a new colour or finish with an old one whenever you feel like it. Throw in a little hole or three. Use thick and thin yarns. Mix pink, yellow, brown and olive. Oh, and stuff the tension square! Basically, just *knit it out. Just tie knots.*

Basic yarn ★ *Ribbing* › 2 strands Peruvian Highland Wool. *Safe, calm basic yarn for breaks in between* › Arwetta or Tilia. *Print yarn* › Mille Colori Baby or Cloud (Yarn types and alternatives, p. 254).

Scrap yarn ★ Varying lengths of thick, thin, smooth or shaggy yarns etc., wound into balls or skeins (p. 234). Or simply lots of balls or skeins of leftover yarns that you already have.

Size ★ 1 (2) 3 (4) 5 (6) 7 (8) (Size guide, p. 239).

Chest measurement of garment ★ Approx. 100 (105) 110 (115) 120 (125) 130 (135) cm. The measurement is the total circumference measured just under the armhole of the pullover, and on this occasion it serves only as a very rough guide. The numbers are only very rough as you will be mixing different types of yarns and knitting holes. This is important for the tension and therefore for the width and length of the pullover. But just keep calm and carry on reading.

Total length ★ Approx. 55 (58) 61 (64) 67 (70) 73 (77) cm from shoulder to bottom edge. These numbers are just for guidance because the more holes you knit, the longer it will make your work (Length, p. 250). The thickness of the knitting and the different yarns will also vary. See above, under Chest measurement.

Yarn requirement ★ *With single-layer ribbing* › at least 2 (2) 2 (2) 2 (3) 3 (3) balls Peruvian Highland Wool. *With rollneck* › at least 3 (3) 3 (3) 4 (4) 4 (4) balls Peruvian Highland Wool. In addition, at least 1 ball Tilia, Arwetta, Cloud and/or Mille Colori Baby. At least 100 g scrap yarn, depending on what you want to knit (Estimating yarn requirements, p. 250).

Needles ★ Circular needle size 10, 80 cm (for front, back and yoke), dpn size 10 (for sleeves, if you are not knitting with Magic Loop, p. 239), circular needle size 7, 60 cm (for ribbing), dpn size 7 (for cuffs, if you are not knitting with Magic Loop), crochet hook size 7 (for assembly).

Tension square ★ Approx. 10-11 sts and 13-15 rows St st with different yarns on needle size 10 = 10 x 10 cm. If the gauge is wrong, try with thicker or thinner needles. Remember: Your gauge will vary if you mix different types of yarn (Tension, p. 239).

Remember the days when you didn't know rules existed? When you could do anything you wanted because there was no wrong or right – unless a grown-up told you, of course? Back then, we had no filters or restrictions. We were free to explore the world and experiment with things, without feeling guilty or embarrassed, and without all the baggage of responsibility that adults lug around with them. Remember when you used to try out colours just because they looked yummy? Or just had to climb the highest tree to look down? When the whole world was just this huge, undiscovered adventure? I would love you to rediscover your inner child now. I know it's in there somewhere. You just have to knit your way through to it!

You can knit the *Inner Child Sweater* however you want – whenever you want, too. When I was a kid, I was good at doing whatever I felt like. But as I grew up, I pushed my wishes and impulses to the back of my mind more and more. They became more and more hidden. But now it's time to rediscover them.

The *Inner Child Sweater* is all about feeling the same, innocent desire to experiment as you did back then. It's about tapping into your inner child and sensing that desire through your

>

It's actually not supposed to be nice.

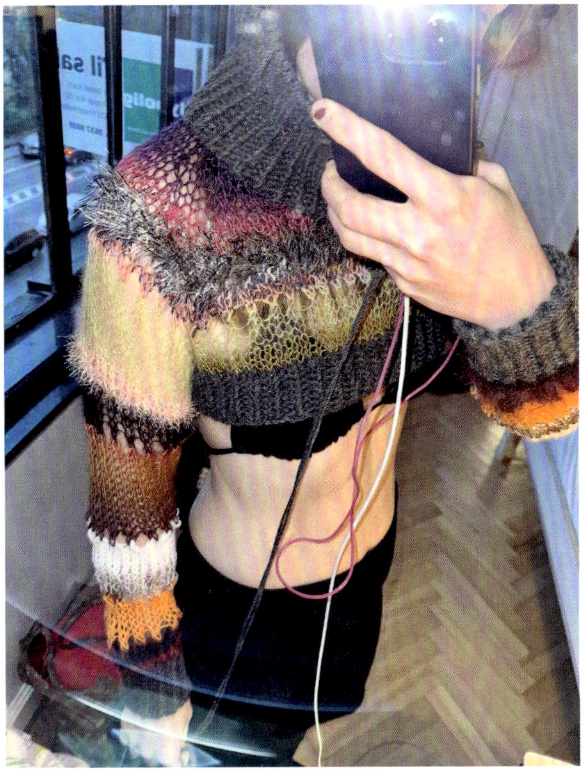

Ribbed cuffs (the classic way) and a very short *Inner Child* crop top with an oversized rollneck in anthracite.

Ribbed cuffs (with thumb hole).

knitting, colours, materials and techniques. Grant yourself the pleasure of reliving that challenging, exciting, intoxicating and – possibly – forbidden freedom again, even if it's only for a short moment.

Sure, back then we definitely needed the guidance and standards of adults. But now your ribbing can be your safety net instead: let that be the grown-up that keeps everything together and prevents any major disasters from happening to you as you let your creativity run free.

You can knit whatever pullover, shrug, crop top or dress you never knew you needed. Knit the front and back as long or short as you like. Add a ribbed neck or rollneck. Personally, I like to put thumb holes into my cuffs – like the ones my pullovers used to have when I was little! Knit holes in patterns or randomly – however the mood takes you. One, two, three, four, or an entire row or round of holes.

It might be a bit tricky, but no matter. I mean, growing up was tricky too, right?

Basic instructions

Front and back ★ Cast on 100 (104) 108 (112) 116 (120) 124 (128) sts using double strand of basic yarn on circular needle size 7. At beg of rnd, place marker. Close to form a rnd. Continue in rib (k1 tbl, p1) in rnds. *Round 1* › Work 50 (52) 54 (56) 58 (60) 62 (64) sts in rib, place marker = side of pullover. Work 5 (5) 6 (6) 7 (7) 8 (8) cm in rib. Switch to circular needle size 10 and continue in rnds in St st in different yarn. Work straight up, go a bit crazy, try it on, have a crisis, feel better, try stuff out, don't give a stuff about standards, cut off and tie knots until your work measures 30 (32) 34 (36) 38 (40) 42 (44) cm including ribbing (if you are knitting a standard-length pullover. If you are making a dress or shrug, simply knit a longer or shorter length.) On both sides of markers for armhole, cast off 3 (3) 3 (4) 4 (4) 5 (5) sts = 88 (92) 96 (96) 100 (104) 104 (108) sts remain. Cut off yarn and put work aside.

Cuff (classic) ★ Cast on 28 (30) 32 (34) 36 (38) 40 (42) sts with double strand of basic yarn – as with front and back – on dpn size 7 (or circular needle with Magic Loop, p. 239). Work 7 cm in rib (k1 tbl, p1). Now continue with instructions for sleeves.

Cuff (with thumb hole) ★ Cast on 28 (30) 32 (34) 36 (38) 40 (42) sts with double strand of basic yarn – as with front and back – on dpn size 7 (or circular needle with Magic Loop, p. 239). Work 5 rnds in rib (k1 tbl, p1). *Round 6* › Continue in rib until 4 sts before end of rnd. Cast off last 4 sts of rnd and first 4 sts of next rnd = 8 sts in total. It looks nicest if you cast off in rib (k above k, p above p). You now have 20 (22) 24 (26) 28 (30) 32 (34) sts on your needle.

Round 7 › Continue until thumb hole. › At end of rnd, cast on 8 new sts. Distribute across Round 8 as before › 4 sts at end and 4 at beg of next rnd. Voilà. One thumb hole done! Now continue in rib, as before. Where you have cast on the new stitches, there will be a little hole. All I can say is: Relax! Accept it! There are far more holes to come. Whatever. Incorporate newly cast-on sts into ribbing. The rnd now has 28 (30) 32 (34) 36 (38) 40 (42) sts again. Work 10 cm in rib. Now continue with instructions for sleeves.

Sleeves ★ Switch to dpn size 10 (or circular needle with Magic Loop, p. 239) and, with different yarn, continue in rnds in St st. Place marker at beg of rnd. Continue in St st. In 4th rnd after ribbing, inc 1 st (p. 244) on each side of marker at beg of rnd › k2, inc 1, k to last 2 sts, inc 1, k2. Inc in the same way on every 4th rnd 5 times in total = 38 (40) 42 (44) 46 (48) 50 (52) sts. When sleeve measures 44 (44) 46 (46) 46 (46) 48 (48) cm or desired length from wrist to armhole – you may need to try it on – cast off 3 (3) 3 (4) 4 (4) 5 (5) sts on both sides of marker = 32 (34) 36 (36) 38 (40) 40 (42) sts. I always knit sleeves by eye, but do it however you like. Cut off yarn and put work aside. Knit second sleeve in exactly the same way.

Yoke ★ Put all pieces on circular needle size 10, positioning sleeves at armholes of front and back. The rnd now consists of 152 (160) 168 (168) 176 (184) 184 (192) sts. Place marker between right sleeve and back (i.e. the sleeve on the right when your work is laid out on the table with the back facing upwards = beg of rnd.) Take up yarn but don't suddenly start knitting neatly just because you've got to the yoke. Work 1 rnd in St st, placing a marker between each piece = 4 markers, including one at beg of rnd.

In next rnd, work raglan decrease as follows › *k1, k2tog (p. 244), continue in St st until 3 sts remain before marker, SKP (p. 244), k1*. Slip marker from left to right needle, rep from * to * to end of round. Rep every 2 rnds. Continue raglan decreases until 32 (34) 36 (38) 40 (42) 44 (46) sts remain on front. On next rnd without raglan decreases: Cast off middle 6 (6) 8 (8) 8 (10) 10 (10) sts on front for neck hole, continue to end of rnd. Cut off yarn. Move all sts from one needle to the other without knitting them so that you can start the neck hole on the left side of your work, i.e. the side to your left when your work is laid out on the table with the front facing upwards. Now continue in St st in rows. Cast off for neck hole while continuing raglan decreases on RS rows. At beg of next 2 rows, cast off for neck hole *as follows*: › at beg of next row, cast off 2 sts, k to end of row. In next row cast off 2 sts at beg and p to end of row. Don't forget to BUTT (p. 242) the edge stitches, as that will make it easier to pick up sts for rollneck later on. In next 6 rows, cast off 1 st at beg of row in exactly the same way. Continue in St st in rows, with raglan decreases on RS rows, until 2 sts remain before markers on both sides of front. Cast off remaining sts starting from front. Looks risky, I know, but together we can do it! See next chapter for grown-up ribbing.

Crew neck or long rollneck, assembly ★ Neck ribbing › Start in middle of back, with RS facing. Using circular needle size 7, pick up 8 sts knitwise for every 9 sts of work, i.e. skip every 9th st/row. Make sure you have an even number of sts. *For crew neck* › With 2 strands of basic yarn, work 6 rnds in rib (k1 tbl, p1). *Round 7* › Cast off in rib (k above k, p above p). *For high fold-down rollneck* › With 2 strands basic yarn, work approx. 30 cm or desired length in rib (k1 tbl, p1). Cast off in rib (k above k, p above p) and fold rollneck down outwards.

To close armholes, sew or knit together from inside – it needn't look nice. It's not supposed to look nice. Just poke into the stitches you see. Sew in or knot the ends.

RIP guilt and shame.

Barbie Knit

Inner Child Sweater

Use a Barbie Knit to try out different colour combinations or see whether to knit a long or short version for yourself.

Basic yarn ★ *Ribbing* › 1 strand Peruvian Highland Wool (Yarn types and alternatives, p. 254).

Scrap yarn ★ Varying lengths of thick, thin, smooth or shaggy yarns etc., wound into balls or skeins (p. 234). Or just strands of leftover yarns. After all, you don't need much.

Size ★ One size.

Yarn requirement ★ At least 20 g.

Needles ★ Size 4 for ribbing, size 5 for the rest. (It's up to you whether you use circular or straight needles to knit in rows), dpn size 4 for rollneck, crochet hook size 4 for assembly.

Technique ★ Knit holes and switch yarn as described for Inner Child technique (p. 37).

Basic instructions

Front and back ★ Cast on 18 sts in basic yarn on size 4 needles. Continue in rib (k1 tbl, p1). Work 2-4 rows for ribbing. Don't forget to BUTT (p. 242) Switch to size 5 needles and change yarn. Continue in St st using the *Inner Child* technique. Continue until work is desired length, then count rows. *Next row* › BUTT, k4, cast off middle 8 sts, k5. *Next row* › BUTT, p4, cast on 8 new sts (p. 244), p4, k1. Knit same number of rows as for front. Switch to size 4 needles. Continue in rib as for front. Cast off.

Sleeves ★ Knit the sleeves onto the front and back in the same way as for the *Fancy Cardy/ Sweater.* If necessary, see p. 138 for details. Work 12 sts on needle size 5, i.e. 6 sts for each side of seam. BUTT, p 1 row. *Next row* › BUTT, k 1 row. Continue in this way until you have 12 rows of St st. Switch to size 4 needle and basic yarn for ribbing. Work 4 rows in rib. Cast off. Knit second sleeve in exactly the same way.

Assembly ★ Crochet side and sleeve seams together using hook size 4 (p. 248). Knot the ends.

Rollneck ★ Using dpn size 4 and basic yarn, pick up approx. 18 sts around neckline. Work 12 rows in rib. Cast off and fold the rollneck down.

Be who you are.

Instructions

3-Day Sweater/Dress/Top/Skirt

Basic yarn ★ *Safe, calm basic yarn for breaks in between* › Arwetta or Tilia. *Print yarn* › Mille Colori Baby and/or Cloud (Yarn types and alternatives, p. 254)

Scrap yarn ★ Varying lengths of thick, thin, smooth or shaggy yarns etc., wound into balls or skeins (p. 234). Or simply lots of balls or skeins of leftover yarns that you already have.

Size ★ 1 (2) 3 (4) 5 (6) 7 (8) (Size guide, p. 239).

Chest measurement of garment ★ Approx. 41 – 48 (44 – 52) 47 – 55 (50 – 58) 52 – 62 (55 – 65) 58 – 68 (61 – 72) cm.
Measurements refer to your knitted piece in a "not-stretched" state (i.e. laid out flat), not against your body. They refer to the entire circumference of the pullover measured just under the armholes. The numbers I provide give you just a rough – very rough – guide because you will be knitting with different types and thicknesses of yarn, with and without holes. That will make a difference to your tension. I knitted myself a size 3 to produce a piece measuring between 47 and 55 cm when laid out flat. But my chest is about 84 cm, so that's what the knitting will actually stretch to in the end.

Total length ★ This will depend on what you are knitting, of course: maxi-dress, mini-dress, crop top or tube. Whatever it is, you will need to make it longer than the length it will ultimately be because when it is stretched out over your body, it will be shorter. I nearly always extend my dresses after I have finished them. I just pick up stitches along the bottom edge and knit on an extra bit. That's the best way to get the length right. But remember: cast off REALLY loosely (with size 10-12 needles if necessary and with such loose arm movements that people will think you are dancing at a party).

Yarn requirement ★ It's difficult to say exactly how much yarn you will need, but try with › 1-2 balls print yarn (e.g. Mille Colori Baby and/or Cloud), 1-2 balls basic yarn (e.g. Tilia and/or Arwetta) and at least 150 g scrap yarns, depending on what you want to knit. (For more on estimating yarn requirements, see p. 250)

Needles ★ Circular needle size 9, 60 cm (for casting on and off), circular needle size 8, 60 cm (for front and back, yoke and sleeves), crochet hook size 7 (for assembly), (dpn size 4 if making straps).

Tension square ★ Approx. 12-14 sts and 15-19 rows in stocking stitch laid out flat, not stretched, with various yarns on size 8 needles = 10 x 10 cm. That's a pretty wide range, I know, but so that you don't get angry with your knitting or with me, you will need to knit a tension square. Cast on the number of stitches for the size you think you need and knit for about 10 cm with your intended yarns. Measure your work at various points and try it out on the widest parts of your body. If it doesn't look good, try a different size. If the tension square is the wrong size, use thicker of thinner needles (p. 239).

Pullover, dress, tube top or tube skirt? You decide! I came up with this design one warm, Danish summer's day in my parents' garden in my beloved Aalborg. I had just got back from Greenland and was feeling very sensitive, vulnerable and dazed – with no filter, basically. I was also travelling alone with my kids, so as always, I had neither the time nor the space to pack properly. As a result I didn't have any additional clothes to wear, nor a knitting project. What I did have, though, was a couple of balls of yarn and some knitting needles, which I had stuffed into a bag in the hope of finding some time to knit. So, this design is the result of three days of impulse-driven holiday knitting done

>

Great fun, damn chic and goddam sexy.

A *3-Day Dress*. You can also just knit the "body" of this dress and cast off, then knit the sleeves and cast off, and leave out the yoke altogether. Just attach the sleeves to the body by stitching them on right under the armpit. (See photo p. 210)

3-Day Sweater.

with my feet in an inflatable paddling pool, a glass of prosecco and a totally random selection of yarns on my needles. This is Lærke – no filters. I was having time off, full of powerful and difficult experiences, and had an emotional hangover. I just wanted to make something quick, with no strings attached, as it were. This design is a good example of how a bit of curiosity, coincidence, inspiration, simplicity and enthusiasm can go a long way, provided you seize the opportunity. Here and there I fixed a few mistakes, but then tadaah! Here it is, in all its northern-Jutland modesty: great fun to knit, damn chic and goddam sexy to go with it.

Follow the free-style knitting guide that is the *Inner Child* technique (p. 39) and remember: there's no need to be 100 percent about the tension. This design has 'negative ease' (p. 239) and is very stretchy. So, I suggest you knit ten rounds in your size and then try it on rather than starting straight off with a project that goes right down to the floor. This design is very

figure-hugging, but the knitting itself is very flexible and stretches with wear. So, if it looks a bit odd and all long and thin when it's laid out on the table, don't panic!

You can make classic, narrow sleeves or medieval Rapunzel-style ones. And by the way, I decided the sleeves on this would be knitted in rows – just to be kind. I tried out all sorts of things, but knitting thin yarn on big, heavy needles with Magic Loop (p. 239), or with double-pointed needles, was just so annoying that I made an executive decision: the sleeves will be knitted in rows. You will be grateful for it. Believe me.

I prefer to knit both sleeves at the same time because I find it goes quicker. That way, when you're done, you can just sit back without having to think about that last, stupid sleeve that still needs doing. If you remember to do the edge right (with a BUTT stitch, see p. 242), the sleeve seams will be much easier to crochet together. If you are making a sleeveless top, skirt or dress, you can add straps or ties (p. 44) instead. You could also consider reinforcing the top edge with elastic thread (p. 46).

Sometimes something that took you five minutes (or three days) to make is at least as good as something that took you a year. And by the way, with this pattern you don't need to knit ribbing.

Yes, indeed, the *3-Day Sweater/Dress/Top/Skirt* is very figure-hugging. But if you don't like that kind of look and prefer a looser fit, why not make the *Inner Child Sweater* on p. 48 as a dress instead?

Basic instructions

Body of pullover/dress/top/skirt ★ Using circular needle size 9, cast on 58 (62) 66 (70) 74 (78) 82 (86) sts very loosely. If you already know you want to make a super-long dress or skirt, work the first 10-20 cm in St st, with BUTT stitches on the edges, before closing to form a rnd. This will make a really cute slit - and give your legs a bit more room for manoeuvre. You can wear the slit on the side or at the back. If you don't want a slit, mark the beginning and side and close to form a round. Work in St st.

Round 1 › Work 29 (31) 33 (35) 37 (39) 41 (43) sts in St st, place marker = side of garment. Switch to circular needle size 8 and knit to required length. If you are average size, like me, (i.e. 168 cm) and knitting something like a dress, you will need at least 90 cm for a mini and at least 140 cm for a maxi dress. If you are making a tube top or tube skirt, approx. 20-50 cm of length will do. For a sweater you need at least 50-60 cm. Try it out. You can always pick up additional stitches or add extra length at the end if you need to. For a tube skirt or top with a tie around the chest (p. 44), you will need to knit a round of holes approx. 1 cm before casting off. For a top with straps, simply cast off when your knitting is the desired length. Cast off knitwise but very loosely – and you're done. The edge will roll up. Accept it, it's part of the design. You may want to knit straps (p. 44) or reinforce the top edge with elastic thread (p. 46). For a dress/pullover, cast off 3 (3) 3 (4) 4 (4) 5 (5) sts on both sides of marker = 46 (50) 54 (54) 58 (62) 62 (66) sts remaining in the rnd. Cut off yarn and put work aside.

Sleeves (narrow) ★ These are knitted in rows. Don't forget to BUTT (p. 242) or use an alternative edge stitch that will make assembly easier. Using circular needle size 8, cast on 20 (22) 24 (26) 28 (30) 32 (34) sts and work in St st. After 3 cm, *with RS facing*, inc 1 (p. 244) *on both sides* as follows › BUTT, k1, inc 1, k to last 2 sts, inc 1, k2. Rep these incs every 3 cm on RS rows, 5 times in total = 30 (32) 34 (36) 38 (40) 42 (44) sts. Continue until work is 50 cm or desired length. If you have long arms (like me), work an additional 5 cm as your knit will be shorter when it's on your body. *On next RS row* › At beg of next 2 rows cast off 3 (3) 3 (4) 4 (4) 5 (5) sts for armhole. You now have 24 (26) 28 (28) 30 (32) 32 (34) sts on your needle. Cut off yarn and put work aside. Knit second sleeve in exactly the same way.

Sleeves (medieval trumpet style) ★ These are knitted in rows. Don't forget to BUTT (p. 242) or use an alternative edge stitch that will make assembly easier. Using circular needle size 8, cast on 40 (42) 44 (46) 48 (50) 52 (54) sts and work in St st. After 3 cm, *with RS facing,* dec 1 (p. 244) *on both sides* as follows › BUTT, k1, SKP (p. 244), k to last 4 sts, k2tog (p. 244), k2. Rep decs every 4 cm with RS facing 5 times in total = 30 (32) 34 (36) 38 (40) 42 (44) sts. Continue

>

until work is approx. 50 cm or desired length. If you have long arms, knit an additional 5 cm as your knit will be shorter when it's on your body. *On next RS row* › At beg of next 2 rows, cast off 3 (3) 3 (4) 4 (4) 5 (5) sts for armhole. You now have 24 (26) 28 (28) 30 (32) 32 (34) sts on your needle. Cut off yarn and put work aside. Knit second sleeve in exactly the same way.

Yoke of sweater/dress ★ Put all pieces on circular needle size 8, positioning sleeves at armholes of front and back = 94 (102) 110 (110) 118 (126) 126 (134) sts in total. Place marker between right sleeve and back (i.e. the sleeve on the right when your work is laid out on the table with the back facing upwards) = beg of rnd. Take up yarn and work 1 rnd in St st, placing a marker between each piece for the yoke = 4 markers in total, including one at beg of rnd. Knit another 2 rnds in St st. Yep, that's right. Because with this design, there are raglan decreases in every 4th rnd. WHAT?! Yesss! Otherwise the yoke will come out too short. In next rnd, work raglan decrease as follows › *k1, k2tog (p. 244), continue in St st until 3 sts remain before marker, SKP (p. 244), k1*. Slip marker from left to right needle, rep from * to * to end of rnd. Rep on every 4th rnd. Continue raglan decreases until 15 (15) 17 (17) 19 (19) 21 (21) sts remain on front. Work until next rnd without decreases. *Next rnd* › Cast off middle 3 (3) 3 (5) 5 (5) 7 (7) sts of front for neck hole (very loosely and possibly with a thicker needle), continue to end of rnd. Cut off yarn. Move all sts from one needle to the other without knitting them so you can start the neck hole on the left side, i.e. the side to your left when your work is laid out on the table with the front facing upwards. Continue in St st, making raglan decreases in every 4th row (RS facing). Cast off for neck hole while continuing raglan decreases on RS. For neck hole, knit 2 together as follows › BUTT, k2tog, continue until 3 sts before end of row, k2tog, k1. Rep decreases for neck hole with RS facing another 1 (1) 1 (2) 2 (3) 3 (4) times. Don't forget to BUTT the edges – that way, if you can see them at all, at least they will look nicer. Continue in St st in rows, with raglan decreases on RS, until 2 sts remain before markers on both sides of front. Using needle size 9, cast off remaining sts starting from front very, very loosely.

Assembly ★ Sew in or knot the ends. If your knitting has big stitches and thin yarn, sewn-in ends sometimes come out again. So, I recommend tying knots wherever you can (p. 237). Close the sleeve seams by crocheting them together in slip stitch through the front loop with hook size 7. Use a medium-thick yarn (e.g. Peruvian, p. 254). You can crochet up one sleeve, from bottom to sleeve hole, and down the other, from sleeve hole to bottom. This will make your seams look the same – although that's not really necessary. I didn't bother either. To close armholes, sew or knit together from inside. It needn't look nice. It's not supposed to look nice. Just poke into the stitches you see. No one will check if you used the right stitches in the armhole. Absolutely no one. Just close up that hole. Isn't that awesome?! Be proud of your body – and your knit. Show yourself. You're beautiful and you deserve it!

Straps (for tube top or dress) ★ Lay your top or dress out flat on the table. There is no official front or back, so just use the side you like best as the front. *Knit a strap onto the front as follows* › Count 5 (5 (5) 6 (7) 7 (8) 8 sts in from the edge to the middle. From here, with dpn size 4, pick up 2 (2) 2 (3) 3 (4) (4) (4) sts (through both loops). Use a medium-thick yarn for this (e.g. Peruvian, p. 254). Work in St st to create a I-cord. Continue until strap is desired length.

Leave an end of approx. 10 cm, then cut off yarn and cast off. To do this, thread the end into a needle and push the needle clockwise into the sts. Carefully pull tight, knot ends and cut off yarn. Work left strap on front in exactly the same way. If desired, knit straps onto the back as well, which you can then tie with front straps on shoulders (Straps, p. 44-45).

3-Day Sweater/Dress/Top/Skirt

Basic yarn ★ *Safe, calm basic yarn for breaks in between* › Arwetta or Tilia. *Print yarn* › Mille Colori Baby. Yarns for needle size 3-3.5 are best, otherwise mix and match to taste. To change colour, simply cut off the yarn and knot in a new one (Yarn types and alternatives, p. 254).

Scrap yarn ★ Varying lengths of thick, thin, smooth or shaggy yarns etc. for needle size 3-3.5, wound into balls or skeins (p. 234). Or just strands of leftover yarns. After all, you don't need much.

Sizes ★ Barbie (Ken).

Yarn requirement ★ At least 10 g.

Needles ★ Size 3 (It's up to you whether you use circular or straight needles to knit in rows), crochet hook size 3 (for assembly).

Technique ★ Knit holes as desired (see p. 43 for instructions). Knit stripes or the Inner Child technique (p. 37).

Try out stripes, sequins (p. 210), beads (p. 251), holes etc.

Don't forget the BUTT stitch!

Basic instructions

Long skirt or dress ★ Cast on 16 (28) sts with needle size 3 and work St st in rows. Don't forget to BUTT the edges. *For Barbie only* › Inc 1 st on each side every 2.5 cm until you have 24 sts. For Ken knit straight up. Work skirt or dress to desired length in desired pattern. Hold the knit up to Barbie/Ken to get the right length. For skirt cast off tight. For dress cast off loosely.

Top (short or long) ★ Cast on 24 (28) sts with needle size 3 and work in St st in rows. Don't forget to BUTT the edges. Knit a few cm – plus a few more for a longer top. Cast off loosely.

Assembly of top, dress and skirt ★ Double crochet (p. 244) along both edges with hook size 3, pushing hook through both loops of BUTT (p. 242). Then crochet sides together in slip stitch (p. 244) through one loop each time. Leave a little slit at bottom of dress/skirt if you wish.

To make a *3-Day*-anything with beads or sequins, like the ones you see here, check out page 210 to see how it's done.

Chapter 2

Nature vs. Lærke, thoughts on Greenland, and the pullover that was a gesture of reconciliation for my dad but came too late.

JORN

Forgive yourself.

This is the sweater my dad would have been proud of. Oh, how I longed for him to be proud of me! This pullover would have passed the test as it would have had all the practical features to meet his requirements. He would even have accepted the "ridiculous" colour because the pullover fulfils its purpose. And therein lies the conflict: all my life – for as long as I can remember, at least – I have found it important for my clothes to look right. I care if they are "on trend", "cool" and "up to date". Basically, I have always thought in terms of aesthetics. My father thought aesthetics were for losers, though. And he didn't mind saying it. He said it often, in fact. I was ridiculous, he was practical.

My dad loved the great, wild outdoors. He took me on holiday to Norway, even when I was still tiny. All I can remember is brown cheese, heather, him being happy and me being scared stiff of the adders and grass snakes, which I never actually saw. I liked it when he was happy. For many years I thought he loved nature more than he loved me.

In fact, he loved nature so much that he moved to Greenland when I was 15. He wrote me a letter to tell me. To say I was sad would be an understatement. The fact that he was moving away at all almost broke me. And so far away too! I was really upset that he didn't tell me to my face. In his letter he said his main reason for moving was me. I hadn't engaged with his life enough and wasn't interested enough in our relationship. So he felt he had to move to Greenland. I understood he couldn't see any reason to stay in Denmark.

He also told me he was only going for a few years. But he never moved back to Denmark. We rarely spoke on the phone because it was too expensive, but we carried on writing to each other and saw each other once a year – but only for a day, when he was on his summer holidays in Denmark. I never knew when he was coming. He would just call me up out of the blue and say, "I'm here! Can we meet tomorrow?" It was terrible. Every year, from mid-July to mid-August, my system would be in crisis mode. Everything happened on his terms. He often said he hated being in the city I was living in. And nor did he like being in a house where there was no space to walk around. He used to say it was unnatural. I lived in an apartment, by the way. Which made it even harder for us to be together. So, I was constantly dancing to his tune, even though I could feel nothing was ever good enough. I mean, it wasn't Greenland, was it?

I have since reread all the letters and emails we sent each other while I was growing up. Our correspondence is full of accusations, misunderstandings, shame and sacrifices – plus a glimmer of hope. Just a tiny one. In a way, I think we had both given up. We had both resigned ourselves and thought we were too far apart, both physically and mentally. I actually have the feeling we never really had the chance to be close and get to know each other.

It's strange reading those letters again. On the one hand it's so obvious that he loved and missed me. But on the other he just didn't understand that it was him that moved such a terribly long way away from his child, and that my life was going on in Denmark. I carried on growing up and finally became an adult. He just didn't get it and was full of accusations.

When I read the letters, I can really sense how much we missed each other and would both have wished for our time together to be different. Deep down, I still don't understand why he moved several thousand kilometres away from his child. I could never do that. Never. Yet at the same time, thinking about it rationally, I totally get it: he just couldn't feel happy and complete in Denmark.

On several occasions he wrote how, since moving to Greenland, there was no looking back. For me as a child, that was a terrible thing to read. I still find it hard to read now, as a grown-up. What do those words really mean? To be perfectly honest, I still feel so angry and upset when I read them. Why would anyone write something like that to their child when they have just moved almost 3,000 kilometres away?

He often said I should come and visit him in Greenland. There was plenty of opportunity – after all, he lived there for more than 15 years. But I never had the courage to go, for fear of being abandoned, left alone in a country 3,000 kilometres from my safe haven, and dependent on someone I had never been able to depend on before. Even if he did want the best for me, without always knowing what the best actually was.

In the summer of 2022, I finally got the opportunity to go to Greenland as part of a shoot for a TV programme. I don't know what I had expected, but I can say without a shadow of a doubt that it was definitely the most amazing trip and nature experience I have ever had.

I had never been even remotely interested in nature all my life. That's not a very popular thing to say, I know, but to me it was just boring – cold and wet, with not much glitter, fur or fashion. Since visiting Greenland, though, I have changed my mind.

Me in Greenland! The wildest experience ever!

TULUGAQ

Lærke, aged four.

When on a mountain in Norway, always take your top off.

Wherever I went, I was greeted with warmth and generosity. I can't even begin to describe the nature. There's more energy and drama in the Greenland countryside than I have ever seen in a fashion show. Of course, Greenland is something you just have to experience for yourself. But let me tell you: from the moment I got there until a fortnight after I left, I was in tears the whole time. It still makes me cry now, to even think of my visit to Greenland.

At Kangerlussuaq airport I thought I saw him. My dad, that is. I know he is dead, so it can't have been him. But I so wanted it to be him. Imagine I had pulled myself together, taken the opportunity and dared to go and see him while we still had the time and he was still alive. I had finally made it to Greenland. But I was five years too late.

All of Greenland was him: from sensible Fjällräven outdoor trousers and trekking boots to all those solo male travellers with their straggly hair, bushy beards and swaggers. So often I thought I saw him. It was driving me absolutely crazy.

Probably the only time I have been out in nature and photographed. Good job we can change our minds. And buy more practical clothes.

What's more, I didn't want to go back to Denmark anymore. I wanted to stay with my dad instead, even if he wasn't there. I felt so close to him – for the first time in many years. Possibly even for the first time ever. When I went back home, he would disappear from my life again and go back to being a stack of melancholy letters and photos in a box.

In Greenland I suddenly came to understand a little more. I caught a fleeting glimpse of someone I desperately wanted to understand and get to know. When he left me, I don't think he was saying 'no' to me; it's just that he couldn't live without his Greenland. The nature up there was just as much a part of him as his heart or his arms and legs. Just like handicrafts and knitting are a part of me.

We are actually not all that different, my dad and me. Not at all, in fact. He moved to Greenland so he could be complete, to be himself and live his dream. I live mine by telling anyone who will listen, on any street corner, to take up knitting (I even weep for knitting in public) and by working at least 70 hours a week (partly in front of the telly, I'll admit). Both of us are/were prepared to make sacrifices. I just wish he hadn't said it was my fault he left. I carried that message within me for years. And it was hard.

For many years I thought he loved nature more than he loved me. But now I know he didn't. It's just that nature was a part of him, and he was not himself unless he was in amongst it. I don't envy him. It must have been a very difficult decision to make. After all, that was what he did, even if he would never have admitted it. To truly see and experience him, I should have seen and experienced Greenland with him.

In a way, the *Family Sweater* (p. 86) is my special homage to him. Knitting is my language and my way of saying "I love you. I'm not angry anymore. I think that now, I understand better who you were."

The reason I am sitting here writing – even though it is so difficult – is possibly because I still yearn for his recognition. Confirmation is a powerful motivator. That's nothing to be ashamed of. Not at all, in my opinion. Not ever.

When I think of him, myself, us, nature, Greenland and Norway, it always reminds me of Fair Isle knits. And if we were to be united in a jumper, it would have to be hard-wearing, practical, chic, colourful and crazy for us both to like it. To me, that's what the *Family Sweater* is.

A cropped version of the *Family Sweater* with a big rollneck. Not very practical, I know, but who cares?! Instructions on page 86.

This is the pullover my dad would have been proud of. It would be a bridge between us and a gesture of reconciliation, better late than never. That's the kind of thing it makes me think. I wish I had knitted this sweater for him – and he had worn it while he was hiking in the mountains, or at the seaside. Imagine me – in a warm pullover – giving my dad a great big hug as he wears another warm pullover. Maybe even the same one? A real family pullover.

Maybe there is someone in your life who deserves a warm woolly hug? Or maybe you deserve one yourself?

I imagine my father would have seen nature, in all its wildness, as perfect. Just like him. He was the kind of person you couldn't pigeonhole. And maybe that's why the freedom, unpredictability, expansiveness and wildness of Greenland gave him a sense of peace and meaning. Neither my dad nor the nature of Greenland could be tamed, steered or reined in. And what does that remind me of these days? Well, my own relationship to knitting and handicrafts. My relationship with life, in fact.

Confirmation is a powerful motivator. That's nothing to be ashamed of.

My grandma knitted these two jumpers for me and my mum. Love you loads, Mum! Hugs, Lærke.

A Fair Isle pattern all over a sweater. Instructions for the *Fancy Cardy/Sweater* are on p. 132.

A Fair Isle pattern that repeats only across certain sections of the garment. Instructions for the *Family Beanie and Headband* are on p. 9

Fair Isle patterns

Fair Isle is a kind of colour work, also known as jacquard knitting. It took quite a while until I finally tried out Fair Isle as it looked so difficult. But do you know what? It's not at all!

In principle it consists of working with multiple strands all at the same time and switching colour as you go. You knit a few stitches in one colour and a few in the other. And in combination your colours create a pattern. The idea of keeping control of more than one strand might sound scary, but it's actually really good fun!!

With Fair Isle, you can knit patterns into your work to make it your very own. And you can either repeat the pattern all over or just have it in certain places. The *Family Sweater* (p. 86) only has a pattern around the yoke, whereas the *Fancy Cardy/Sweater* (p. 132) is patterned all over.

When you are knitting with more than one colour – Fair Isle with multiple strands, in other words – the strand you are not using just hangs loosely on the back of the work. When you change colour, it becomes your active yarn. The threads across the back of your work are called "floats", and if you can get them just right – as in not too loose and not too tight – then you've found the happy medium. It's very easy to pull the float too tight, in which case you might end up with a pullover that you can't get over your head, or that has strange lumps and

Wait a minute, Callborg.

Wow, the inside looks great, doesn't it?

bumps because the patterned section is too tight. That's not what you want, right? But you might also knit too loose and sloppy because you're trying to keep all those strands under control. I've done both. And you might too.

But don't despair if you find you have to knit a few centimetres until you get the hang of it. With me, success often depends on the needle size. If you are knitting Fair Isle, in general I think it's a good idea to use a thicker needle than the label on the yarn says. That way it won't come out too tight.

After all, there is nothing worse than a tight, lumpy knit that rubs when you wear it. If you are going to all the trouble of juggling multiple strands, at least you want to end up with something decent. But give it a whirl and see what works best for you. And don't get this confused with the tip on page 80, where I advise using a thinner needle to knit a pattern. That's something completely different. Here, we are talking about combining pattern-free stocking stitch with a patterned Fair Isle (star chart) section to create the *Family Sweater*. If you don't switch to a different needle size, it might look out of proportion when you change between plain and pattern. Try it out – but listen more to your heart than to me.

Listen to your heart,

13
ode ligger
Margherita
issonis gener.
Her som lille
pige i prikker,
stjerner, hat og
nethandsker

A band of Fair Isle pattern is great for pullovers with a yoke. Draw a few sketches of your pattern and follow them as you knit (p. 206-207, Creating your own colour chart).

How to knit with multiple yarns

There are various ways of holding your yarns when you knit a coloured pattern. You can either hold both strands in one hand, or one in each hand. Or you can just hold a single yarn at any given time and leave the other one dangling from the back of your work. When you need to use it, you just pick it up and carry on. I use the latter method because that's what works best for me. I tend to be a bit of a fumble-fingers, so for me it is definitely easiest to keep just a single thread going at a time.

The yarns can easily get in a tangle, but there are clever ways of preventing that – plus all manner of gadgets. In my experience, though, the various gadgets are no easy fix. *The way I do it is this*: if things get messy, I untangle the yarns or cut them off and start again. Forget the bullsh*t. Just tie knots.

Whether it's rows or rounds you are knitting, always change colour on the back of your work. That way you will have your floats on the back and your pattern on the front. A lot of people don't like knitting Fair Isle patterns in rows because it means you have to knit the pattern from the back of the work too. Which is not everyone's cup of tea. I kind of get that: it does sound like the kind of thing that could all end in tears, especially if the pattern is complicated. But I don't really like knitting complicated patterns because I can't watch telly while I'm doing it.

For the sake of simplicity, let's call one yarn the main strand and the other one the pattern strand. Typically, your main strand will be the one you use most, the main colour of your work, in other words. Your pattern strand will be the one you are making the actual pattern with. With my knitting patterns, both the main colour and the pattern colour are in basic yarn, but the pattern colour is combined with scrap yarn. For this reason, I refer to the main colour as 'basic yarn 1' and the pattern colour as 'basic yarn 2'. For more on the yarn types used in the different instructions with Fair Isle effects, see pages 86, 92, 96, 100, 126, 132, 142 and 146.

How to hold the yarns so they run evenly along the back of your work

★ When knitting in the main colour, lay the strand over the pattern colour.

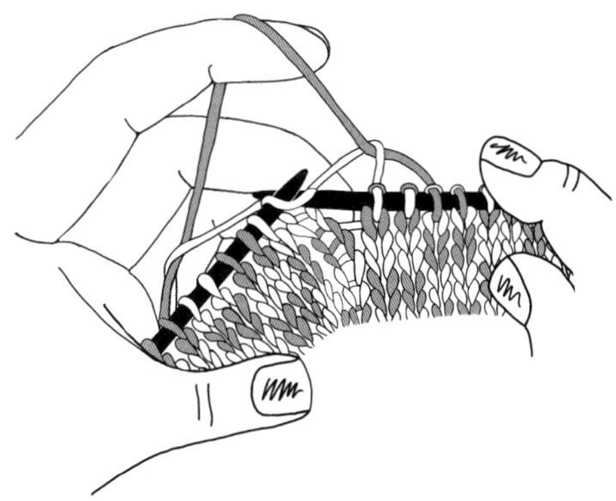

★ When knitting in the pattern colour, lay the strand under the main colour.

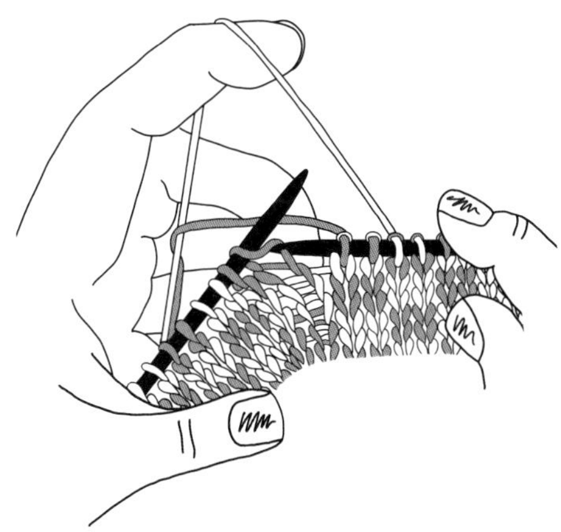

That way you will always knit the same strand from above and below.

>

It's almost as though you are twisting the threads with each other.

Use the same method when you have the wrong side of your work facing you – but this time with the threads in front of your work.

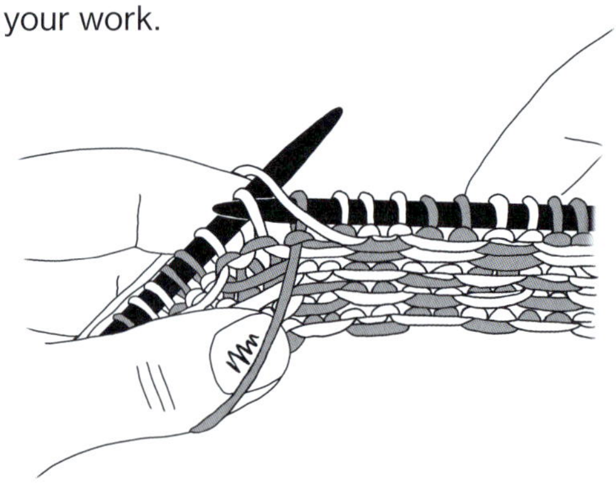

If you find yourself getting confused with all the above and below stuff, you might end up with a tangle. If that happens, just untangle your strands again. Or cut them off and knot them (p. 237). No big deal.

How to run your passive strand across your work

Your active strand is the one you are knitting with. The passive one just hangs from the back of your work. To switch to your passive strand, pull it over to where you want to pick it up – but not too tight and not too loose either.

If your passive strand has to span more than about five to seven stitches, you will need to "lock" the float on the back of your work so it doesn't hang loose. To do this, wrap the passive strand once around the active one so that it's more or less being held up to the back of your work. Just lay it around the active thread, but don't knit it. How many or few stitches you want between each lock is entirely up to you. Personally, I have a limit of seven stitches. I don't lock with just six stitches (for instance, in the *Fancy* instructions on p. 126-147). But some people like a lock after just four stitches. So, you really need to just see what works for you.

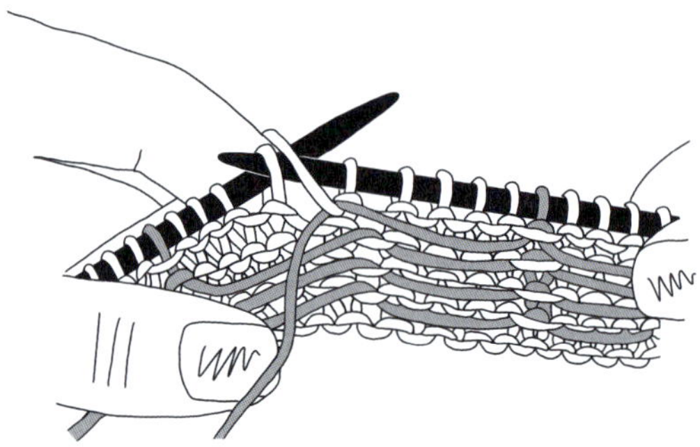

Make sure you tension the main colour regularly when you continue after wrap-ping your pattern colour around it.

How to add a new colour

You can add a new colour with the front or the back of your work facing you. If you are starting your new colour on the first stitch on your needle, integrate it straight after the BUTT and knot or sew in the end along the edge of your knitting. If you are starting a new colour in the middle of a row/round – as happens in a number of knitting patterns in this book (p. 86-100) – here's what to do:

With the right side of your work facing you

★ Knit to where you need to change colour. Lay the new colour over the old one, with the tail end pointing to the left.

BLAH BLAH

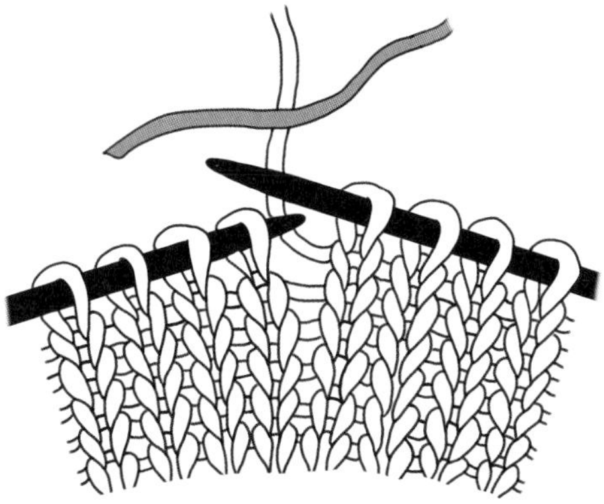

★ Wind the two threads around each other so that the old colour lies over the new one.

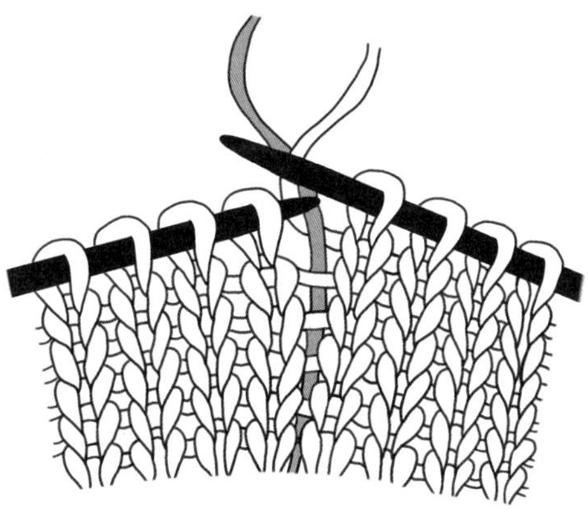

BLAH BLAH
BLAH BLAH

Knit with the new colour, giving the end of the strand a slight tug to tighten the stitches where you switched yarn.

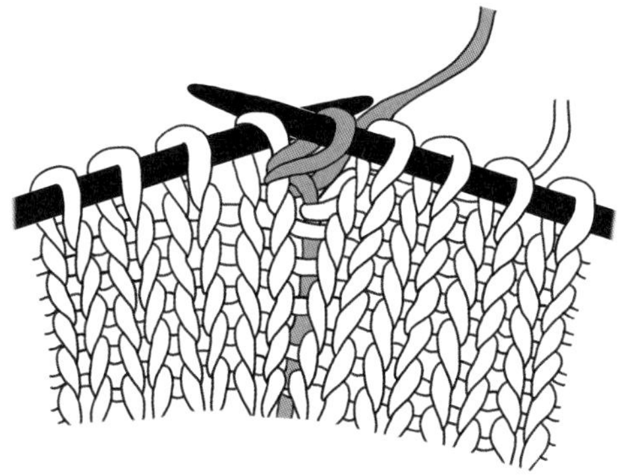

Do the same with the wrong side of your work facing you. Here's how:

★ Wrap the two yarns around each other.

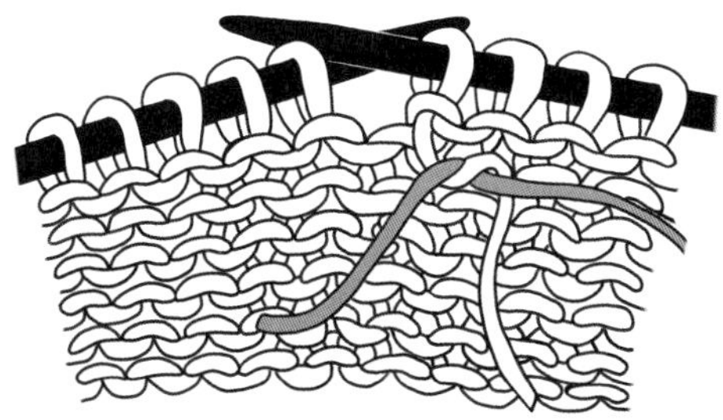

★ Purl the next stitch in your new colour.

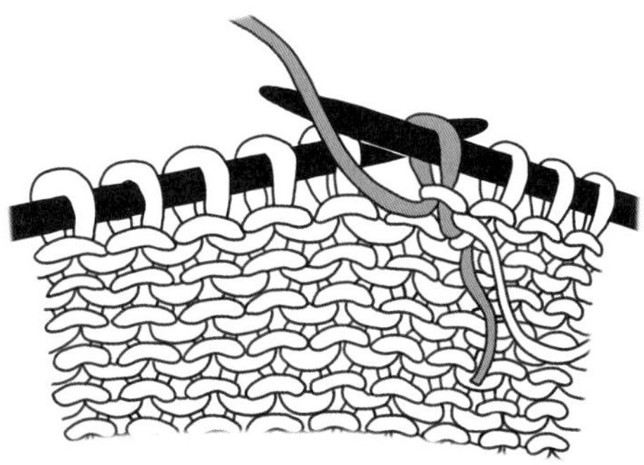

Tips for Fair Isle knitting

Try it out first. If you have never done Fair Isle knitting before, give yourself the time to learn how it's done – before casting on for a floor-length coat! As with any other technique, the way you knit Fair Isle really depends on what works for you. Do you like to knit tight? Or do you prefer things loose? Will you wrap the threads around each other manually or drape them over your index finger? For example, I learned the basics of Fair Isle when I was knitting a long dress with different patterns on the front and back on size 3.5 needles for the Hønsestrik movement. I wouldn't recommend that. Not even to my worst enemy. But how about trying it out on a little Barbie Sweater (p. 100 and p. 146)?

Keep an eye on how tight your knitting is. With Fair Isle you are using multiple strands, so your work will automatically be twice as thick (because you have all the floats on the back). So, it is often better to use needles that are one size bigger than the label on the yarn says. The knitting patterns in this book all take the floats into account, so don't worry. But say you are using two yarns where the recommendation is size 5 needles. If I were you, I would go either a half or a whole size up and use size 5.5 or 6 needles.

Sometimes your Fair Isle section will have areas that are larger or smaller, or that pucker or go wavy. That means you probably haven't been taking enough care over your floats because you were too busy watching the telly. It happens to me all the time. But fear not. Often, you can do quite a lot by pulling or tugging at the pattern. The risk of knitting some bits less carefully than others is quite high, but if you give your work a (gentle) tug both lengthways and widthways, it will probably sort itself out. A bit, at least.

If you are knitting Fair Isle in rows, it may help to do the penultimate stitch on your needle in plain using both the pattern colour and the main colour together. That will lock both strands in place and make them easier to use in the next row. As I say, it's not imperative, but it's a good option if you want a really neat finish.

The *Family Sweater* (p. 86) has a Fair Isle pattern only on the yoke. I tend to knit the patterned section slightly more loosely than the rest of the pullover. It's probably psychological: I am SOOO scared of it puckering that I knit loosely enough for the patterned stitches to actually be bigger than the stitches in the rest of the sweater. That's why I always use needles one size smaller than for the rest of the garment. Now there's a nugget of advice for you! So, basically: go down a needle size for Fair Isle if the rest of the pullover is unicoloured because it will give you a more even result. If you forget, don't worry – I will remind you to change needle in the instructions every time you switch between uni- and multicolour Fair Isle knitting. Whether or not you will actually have this problem, nobody knows. I know a lot of lucky people who manage just fine!

Normally the bit that takes the most concentration is the first few rows of the pattern. That's because you are not familiar with it yet, so you will probably make quite a few mistakes. If you do, you will have to go back and put it right. Because a single wrong stitch in Fair Isle sends everything out of kilter and will destroy the whole thing. So, switch off the *Gilmore Girls* and knit your first few rows without. Until you have got the hang of the pattern. Oh, the number of times I have confused that TV account! And it annoys me every time!

If you need to find your way across multiple rows in a long pattern, use something like a Post-It to help you read the colour chart. Every time you have finished a row, move the Post-It up a line. That way you will always know what row of the colour chart you are on.

>

The *Let It All Hang Out Scarf* (p. 218).

And then there's the question of pattern dominance. "What on earth is that?" I hear you ask. "Good question," I reply. I am not entirely sure myself. It probably has something to do with which colour is the dominant one in your pattern. It depends on which colours you have chosen, of course, but in my experience, it tends to be the darker colour. Take a look at the pictures opposite. Do you want your main colour to dominate or your pattern colour? In the end it doesn't matter: it just depends on what you like and differs from one design to the next. Sometimes pattern dominance in the main colour looks best. Sometimes not. A stupid answer, I know. But the pictures show clearly how it works, and you should just do what works best for you. I don't know everything. No one knows everything.

Last but not least I would like to say that, in my opinion, Fair Isle patterns look best when you use different types of yarn. It heightens the contrast and dynamism. It's like a dialogue between the yarns. Fair Isle is all about knitting with different elements (i.e. different colours), but if you knit the whole thing in the same type of yarn, it can easily look a bit boring. So, let rip! Bring out the shapes by heightening the contrasts.

Dress with Fair Isle patterns, inspired by the Hønsestrik movement, plus lots of different, really beautiful swatches.

Colour charts for dummies

A colour chart maps out how to knit a Fair Isle pattern. Each box represents one stitch, and each row of the chart represents one row/round of knitting. The pattern it shows is repeated x number of times to fill the whole row/round – and is therefore known as a "repeat".

The filled-in boxes in the colour chart represent the stitches you are going to knit in your pattern colour. The empty boxes are your main colour.

I draw my colour charts on squared paper – with *square* boxes. But in knitting, stitches are not square. They are wider than they are high. So, if you think a pattern looks a bit long on the chart, don't worry. It's because my sketch on squared paper takes the shape of actual stitches into account so that the final knit will look good.

Colour charts usually start with the right side of the work facing you – unless stated otherwise. So, the first stitch of the colour chart that you knit will be the one in the bottom right-hand corner. The way you read the colour chart will depend on whether you are knitting rows or rounds. If you are knitting rows, you will need to read the chart from right to left on right-side rows, and left to wrong-side rows. After you finish knitting a row, you move on to the next row up on the chart.

If you are knitting in rounds, you will need to read the chart from right to left the entire time because you have the right side of your work facing you throughout. So, when you have repeated the pattern the number of times it says in the instructions, you will need to start on the next row up on the colour chart and knit that from right to left, again with the right side of your work facing you.

The colour charts in the instructions in this book are designed to be read as repeats. In other words, what you see in the chart must be repeated over and over until you have completed your round or row. A repeat can also be repeated upwards. In the *Family Sweater* (p. 86) it is only repeated across, all the way round the pullover, whereas in *Fancy* (p. 126-147) it is repeated not just around the sweater but up the sweater as well. To repeat upwards, all you do is finish the first pattern completely and then go back down to the bottom right-hand corner of the chart and start again. That way the repeats will be one above the other. Voilà!

Fancy Bag, instructions on p. 126.

Colour charts A and B for the *Family Sweater* (grown-ups and kids, p. 86 and 92).

Colour chart C for *Family Beanie + Family Headband* (p. 96).

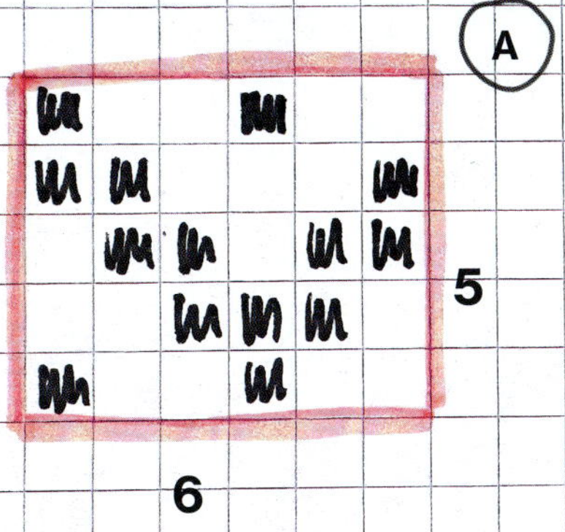

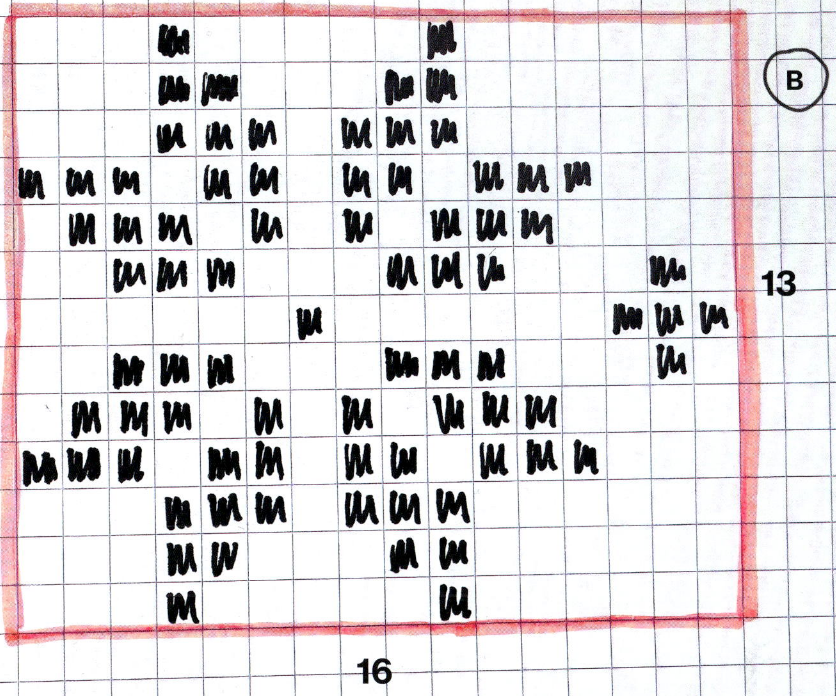

Family Sweater (grown-ups and kids), p. 86 + 92

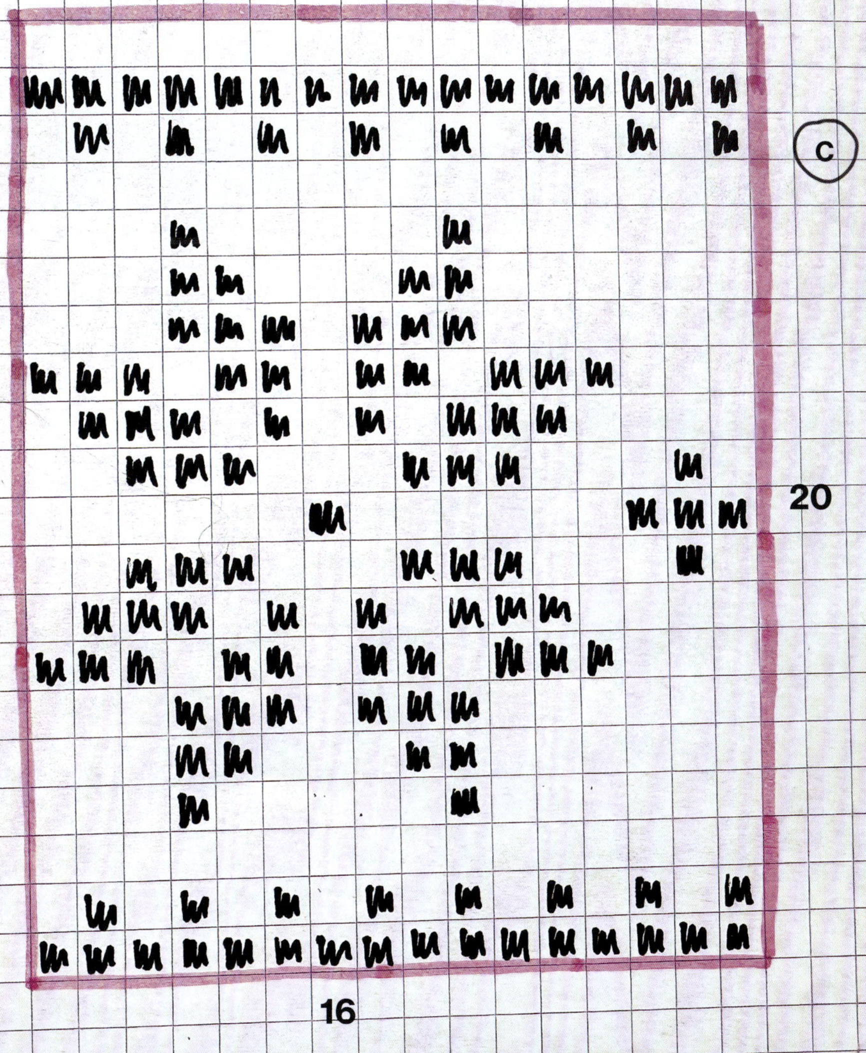

Family Beanie + Family Headband, p. 96

Instructions

I'm gonna knit him a sweater he can't refuse!

Family Sweater (grown-ups)

Basic yarn ★ *Basic yarn 1 (main colour)* › 1 strand Fritidsgarn alone, or 1 strand Peruvian Highland Wool plus 1 strand Arwetta or Tilia. *Basic yarn 2 (pattern colour)* › 3 strands Tilia or 3 strands Arwetta or 1 strand Peruvian Highland Wool plus 1 strand scrap yarn (Yarn types and alternatives, p. 254).

Scrap yarn ★ Varying lengths of thick, thin, smooth or shaggy yarns etc., wound into balls or skeins (p. 234). Or simply lots of balls or skeins of leftover yarns that you already have.

Size ★ 1 (2) 3 (4) 5 (6) 7 (8) (Size guide, p. 239).

Chest measurement of garment ★ Approx. 90 (95) 100 (105) 110 (115) 120 (125) cm. This measurement is the total circumference measured just under the armhole of the pullover.

Total length ★ Approx. 54 (56) 58 (60) 62 (64) 66 (68) cm from shoulder to bottom edge if you are knitting measurements in these instructions. For a short, very short or longer version of the knit, adapt the length accordingly before the armhole (Length, p. 250).

Yarn requirement ★ *Basic yarn 1* › At least 5 balls Frtitidsgarn or Peruvian Highland Wool and at least 3 balls Tilia or Arwetta. *Basic yarn 2* › At least 2 balls Tilia (knit 3 strands) or 2 balls Arwetta (knit 3 strands) or 2 balls Peruvian Highland Wool (knit one strand). *Scrap yarn* › At least 30 g.

Needles ★ Circular needle size 7, 80 cm (for front/back and yoke), dpn size 7 (for sleeves, if you are not knitting with Magic Loop, p. 239), circular needle size 6, 60 cm (for ribbing and neck hole), dpn size 6 (for cuffs and pattern on sleeves, if you are not knitting with Magic Loop), circular needle size 6, 80 cm for pattern (on front/back and yoke), crochet hook size 6-7 (for assembly).

Tension square ★ Approx. 12 sts and 17-18 rows St st with needles size 7 = 10 x 10 cm. (Tension, p. 239). If your gauge is different, use thicker or thinner needles.

Colour charts A + B, page 85.

The *Family Sweater* is the perfect pullover. Or at least, as perfect as I can make it. It's a born classic because it's quite simply, well, classic – but still super-fresh. This is the jumper my dad would have been proud of. It would have made him happy. A real family pullover.

The *Family Sweater* is really versatile, and you can make it for all your family and friends. All you have to do is adapt the length of the sleeves to fit the intended wearer. Knit the front and back long, medium or – for a crop top or shrug – really short. You can make the sleeves with or without patterns. My darling Sune prefers his without (p. 87).

The *Family Sweater* is knitted in one main colour, with a zigzag and star edging in the pattern colour plus one stand of scrap yarn. Ideally, your pattern colour should contrast nicely with the main colour. How strongly is for you to decide. I recommend knitting a swatch to try out the colours together (or maybe a *Barbie Family Sweater*, p. 100). There was a time when I was quite often disappointed with the way combinations I thought would be awesome actually turned out. They were just totally vanilla. Remember to use black and white scraps as well because they create a really nice contrast. Use mohair (3 strands of Tilia), merino (3 strands of Awetta) or classic, untreated wool (1 strand of Peruvian) as your pattern colour and combine it with some scrap.

>

POLO
DRIK MED RESPEKT

adidas

Full-length with pale pink as the main colour and purple + scraps as the pattern colour.

Alternatively, mix things up a bit. You're the boss. And it's up to you to decide which side will be the front or back as well – because the yoke doesn't have a specific neck hole. Because you are using scrap for the stars, the two sides will look different. But you can just choose the one with the nicest colours for the front! But don't deliberate for too long because as soon as you start wearing your jumper, the shape will start to adapt to fit your body.

By the way, the patterned sections are knitted with needles one size smaller than for the rest of the pullover. Often, people tend to knit their Fair Isle patterns looser (or sloppier!). I do, at least. It's probably psychological: I am SOOO scared of pulling too tight that I end up with everything too loose. Other people knit their Fair Isle tighter. So, my advice would be to knit a sample first. Even though it's annoying. But it does help you find out how tightly you knit. You can also see if the colours you have chosen look good together. Maybe, like me, you have a partner (or other person) who knows exactly what they want the jumper to look like and *definitely do not want* the zigzag border at the bottom of the front, back and sleeves. If that's the case, switch to bigger needles straight after the ribbing and do the five rounds without the pattern. With this pullover, by the way, I didn't lock the floats even though they sometimes extend across quite a lot of stitches. But it's up to you, of course. Do what you think is best. (Floats, p. 78)

Basic instructions

Front and back ★ Cast on 108 (114) 120 (126) 132 (138) 144 (150) sts using 1 strand basic yarn 1 and circular needle size 6. Place marker at beg of rnd = side of pullover. Close to form rnd and continue in rib (k1 tbl, p1). *Round 1* › Work 54 (57) 60 (63) 66 (69) 72 (75) sts, place marker = other side of pullover. Work 5 (5) 6 (6) 7 (7) 8 (8) cm in rib. Switch to needle size 7 and work 1 rnd in St st. Switch back to needle size 6 (if you knit Fair Isle looser than St st, p. 80, if not, don't switch). *Next rnd* › Work in pattern as in colour chart A with basic yarn 1 as main colour and basic yarn 2 (don't forget scrap strand!) as pattern colour, for a total of 5 rnds. When pattern in colour chart A is complete, switch to circular needle size 7 and continue in St st until work is approx. 30 (32) 34 (36) 38 (40) 42 (44) cm or desired length. If you are knitting, say, a shrug, a total of 7-20 cm will do. For a crop top, knit approx. 12-25 cm. For an extra-long knit (e.g. a guy's sweater) add more length.

For the armholes, on both sides of markers, cast off 2 (2) 3 (3) 4 (4) 5 (5) sts = 100 (106) 108 (114) 116 (122) 124 (130) sts remaining in rnd. Cut off yarn and put work aside.

Sleeves (with or without pattern) ★ Cast on (36) 36 (36) 36 (36) 36 (36) 36 sts using 1 strand basic yarn 1 and dpn size 6 (or circular needle with Magic Loop, p. 239). Place marker at beg of rnd. Close to form rnd and continue in rib (k1 tbl, p1). Switch to dpn size 7 (or circular needle with Magic Loop) and work 1 rnd St st. Switch back to circular needle size 6 (if you knit Fair Isle looser than St st and you changed needle on the front and back).

This one is mega-cropped (for the same sweater as a half-long version in black, see p. 246). Made with brown Fritidsgarn as the main colour and pale brown mohair + scrap as the pattern colour.

Work pattern as in colour chart A for a total of 5 rnds. If you don't want a pattern around the bottom, work 5 rnds on circular needle size 7. When pattern in colour chart A is complete, switch to dpn or circular needle size 7 and continue in St st. In 2nd rnd after pattern, inc 1 st (p. 244) *on both sides of markers* as follows › k2, inc 1, k to last 2 sts, inc 1, k2. Rep this inc on every 4th rnd 4 (4) 6 (6) 8 (8) 10 (10) times in total = 44 (44) 48 (48) 52 (52) 56 (56) sts. Continue until sleeve is approx. 44 cm long or desired length from wrist to armhole. If you want to knit a different sleeve length, this is where you can lengthen/shorten it. Try the sleeve on if you need to. For armhole, on either side of markers cast off 2 (2) 3 (3) 4 (4) 5 (5) sts = 40 (40) 42 (42) 44 (44) 46 (46) sts in total remaining in rnd. Cut off yarn and put work aside. Knit second sleeve in exactly the same way.

Yoke ★ Put all pieces on circular needle size 7, positioning sleeves at armholes on front and back = 180 (186) 192 (198) 204 (210) 216 (222) sts in total. Place marker between right sleeve and back (i.e. the sleeve on the right when your work is laid out on the table with the back facing upwards) = beg of rnd. Use 1 strand basic yarn 1 and work 1 rnd in St st, placing a marker between each piece for yoke = 4 markers in total. In next rnd, work raglan decrease as follows › k1, k2tog (p. 244), continue in St st until 3 sts remain before marker, SKP (p. 244), k1*. Slip marker from left to right needle, rep from * to * to end of rnd and in every second rnd a total of 2 (3) 4 (4) 5 (6) 7 (7) times = 164 (162) 160 (166) 164 (162) 160 (166) sts. *Next rnd* › dec 4 (2) 0 (6) 4 (2) 0 (6) sts evenly (p. 244). You now have 160 sts (all sizes). Switch to circular needle size 6 (if you changed for the Fair Isle pattern) and continue as in colour chart B (for 13 rnds in total).

Next rnd › *Work 14 sts, SKP *, rep from * to * to end of rnd = 150 sts. Continue as in colour chart A (for a total of 5 rnds). Switch to needle size 7 and work 1 rnd in St st. Now start decreasing for neck in every second round to end of work. At beg of round, work as follows › *k2tog, 13 sts St st*, rep from * to * to end of rnd = 140 sts. Work 1 rnd in St st. Next rnd › *12 sts St st, SKP*, rep from * to * to end of rnd = 130 sts. Work 1 rnd in St st. Next rnd › *SKP, 11 sts St st*, rep from * to * to end of rnd = 120 sts. Work 1 rnd in St st. Next rnd › *10 sts St st, SKP*, rep from * to * to end of rnd = 110 sts. Work 1 rnd in St st. Next rnd › *SKP, 9 sts St st*, rep from * to * to end of rnd = 100 sts. Work 1 rnd in St st. Next rnd › *8 sts St st, SKP*, rep from * to * to end of rnd = 90 sts. Work 1 rnd in St st. Next rnd › *SKP, 7 sts St st*, rep from * to * to end of rnd = 80 sts. Work 1 rnd in St st. Switch to circular needle size 6 for neck ribbing.

Neck and assembly ★ For short, single-layer neck ribbing › On circular needle size 6, work in rib (k1 tbl, p1) in rnds. After 5 cm cast off (not too tightly) in rib (k above k, p above p). For roll-neck › On circular needle size 6, work in rib (k1 tbl, p1 tbl) in rnds. After 30 cm cast off loosely in rib (k above k, p above p). Sew or crochet armholes together from inside. Sew in or knot the ends.

Instructions

Family Sweater (kids)

Lars. A cool boss. Knitted with black as the main colour and anthracite + scrap as the pattern colour.

Basic yarn ★ *Basic yarn 1 (main colour)* › 1 strand Peruvian Highland Wool. *Basic yarn 2 (pattern colour)* › 2 strands Tilia or 1 strand Arwetta plus 1 strand scrap yarn (Yarn types and alternatives, p. 254).

Scrap yarn ★ Varying lengths of thick, thin, smooth and shaggy yarns, wound to balls or skeins (p. 234). Or simply lots of balls or skeins of leftover yarns that you already have. Ideally, use yarns that suit needle size 3-4 so that the pattern doesn't come out wavy.

Size ★ 2 (4) 6 (8) 10 (12) years (Size guide, p. 239).

Chest measurement of garment ★ Approx. 67 (70) 74 (77) 81 (84) cm. The measurement is the total circumference measured just under the armhole.

Total length ★ Approx. 37 (41) 46 (50) 55 (60) cm from shoulder to bottom edge, if you are knitting measurements as in these instructions. To knit a longer version, e.g. for a dress, or a shorter version, knit longer or shorter up to the armhole.

Yarn requirement ★ *Basic yarn 1* › At least 2 (3) 4 (4) 5 (5) balls Peruvian Highland Wool. *Basic yarn 2* › 1 ball Tilia or 1 ball Arwetta for all sizes. *Scrap yarn* › At least 20 g.

Needles ★ Circular needle size 5, 60 cm (for front/back and yoke), dpn size 6 (for sleeves, if you are not knitting with Magic Loop, p. 239), circular needle size 4, 40 cm (for ribbing, pattern and neck hole), dpn size 4 (for cuffs and pattern, if you are not knitting with Magic Loop), crochet hook size 4 (for assembly).

Tension ★ Approx. 17 sts and 24-27 rows St st with needles size 5 = 10 x 10 cm. (Tension, p. 239). If your gauge is different, use thicker or thinner needles.

Colour chart A + B, p. 85.

Sooo cute, huh? This is a kiddies' version of the *Family Sweater*, but on thinner needles and made with thinner yarn than the grown-up version. It's the kind of pullover you dream of your kids loving, but of course they don't. At least, mine don't. *Sigh*. This little sweater is knitted with one strand of basic yarn in the main colour and one strand of basic yarn in the pattern colour plus one strand of scrap yarn. The basic yarn for the pattern colour can be something like mohair or merino. For best results, use scrap yarn suitable for needle sizes 3-4. That way, you won't end up with your pattern going wavy.

Before you start, read about the grown-up version of the *Family Sweater* (p. 86), as there are some important tips. And don't forget to knit the patterned sections on a thinner needle if you tend to be a sloppy knitter. And yes, you need to cast on the same number of stitches as for the grown-up version. The difference is, this kiddies' jumper is done on thinner needles.

The kind of pullover you dream of your kids loving, but of course they don't.

Brown as main colour with pink + scrap as pattern colour.

Basic instructions

Front and back ★ Cast on 114 (120) 126 (132) 138 (144) sts using 1 strand basic yarn and circular needle size 4. Place marker at beg of round = side of pullover. Close to form rnd and continue in rib (k1 tbl, p1). *Round 1* › Work 57 (60) 63 (66) 69 (72) sts, place marker = other side of pullover. Work 4 (4) 4 (5) 5 (5) cm in rib. Work 1 rnd is St st (still on size 4 needle). *Next rnd* › Work in pattern as in colour chart A with basic yarn 1 as main colour and basic yarn 2 (don't forget scrap strand!) as pattern colour, for a total of 5 rnds. When pattern in colour chart A is complete, switch to circular needle size 5 and continue in St st until work is approx. 20 (23) 26 (30) 33 (37) cm or desired length. If you want to make a longer garment, add extra rows here. On both sides of markers, cast off 4 (4) 5 (5) 6 (6) sts for armhole = 98 (104) 106 (112) 114 (120) sts remaining. Cut off yarn and put work aside.

Sleeves ★ Cast on (36) 36 (42) 42 (48) 48 sts using 1 strand basic yarn 1 and dpn size 4 (or circular needle with Magic Loop, p. 239) Place marker at beg of rnd. Close to form rnd and work 4 (4) 4 (5) 5 (5) cm in rib (k1 tbl, p1). Work 1 rnd in St st (still on size 4 dpn or circular needle with Magic Loop). *Next rnd* › Work pattern as in colour chart A for a total of 5 rnds. When pattern in colour chart A is complete, switch to dpn or circular needle size 5 and continue in St st. In 2nd rnd after pattern, inc 1 st (p. 244) *on both sides of markers* as follows › k2, inc 1, k to last 2 sts, inc 1, k2. Rep this inc on every 5th rnd 5 times in total = 46 (46) 52 (52) 58 (58) sts. Continue until sleeve is approx. 22 (25) 28 (32) 35 (38) cm or desired length from wrist to armhole. If you want to knit a different sleeve length, this is where you can add/shorten it. Try the sleeve on if you need to. On both sides of markers, cast off 4 (4) 5 (5) 6 (6) sts for armhole = 38 (38) 42 (42) 46 (46) sts remaining. Cut off yarn and put work aside. Knit second sleeve in exactly the same way.

Now, relax.

White as the main colour with beige + scraps as the pattern colour.

Yoke ★ Put all pieces on circular needle size 5, positioning sleeves at armholes on front and back = 174 (180) 190 (196) 206 (212) sts in total. Place marker between right sleeve and back (i.e. the sleeve on the right when your work is laid out on the table with the back facing upwards) = beg of rnd. Take 1 strand basic yarn 1 and work 1 rnd in St st, placing a marker between each piece for yoke = 4 markers in total. In next rnd, work raglan decrease as follows › *k1, k2tog (p. 244), continue in St st until 3 sts remain before marker, SKP (p. 244), k1*. Slip marker from left to right needle, rep from * to * to end of rnd and in every second rnd a total of 2 (3) 4 (5) 6 (7) 8 (9) times = 158 (156) 158 (156) 158 (156) sts. Next rnd › Inc 2 (4) 2 (4) 2 (4) sts evenly (p. 244), either on both sleeves (if increasing 2 sts) or on both sleeves plus front and back (if increasing 4 sts). You now have 160 sts (all sizes). Switch to circular needle size 4 (if you changed for the Fair Isle pattern) and continue as in colour chart B (for 13 rnds in total). Next rnd › *Work 14 sts, SKP*, rep from * to * to end of rnd = 150 sts. Continue as in colour chart A (for a total of 5 rnds). Switch to needle size 5 and work 1 rnd in St st. Now start decreasing for neck in every second round to end of work. At beg of rnd, work as follows › *k2tog, work 13 sts in St st*, rep from * to * to end of rnd = 140 sts. Work 1 rnd in St st. Next rnd › *Work 12 sts in St st, SKP*, rep from * to * to end of rnd = 130 sts. Work 1 rnd in St st. Next rnd › *SKP, 11 sts in St st *, rep from * to * to end of rnd = 120 sts. Work 1 rnd in St st. Next rnd › *10 sts St st, SKP*, rep from * to * to end of rnd = 110 sts. Work 1 rnd in St st. Next rnd › *SKP, 9 sts St st*, rep from * to * to end of rnd = 100 sts. Work 1 rnd in St st. Next rnd › *Work 8 sts St st, SKP*, rep from * to * to end of rnd = 90 sts. Work 1 rnd in St st. Next rnd › *SKP, 7 sts St st*, rep from * to * to end of rnd = 80 sts. Work 1 rnd in St st. Switch to circular needle size 4 for neck ribbing.

Neck and assembly ★ On circular needle size 4, work in rib (k1 tbl, p1) in rnds. After 3 (3) 3 (4) 4 (4) cm cast off (not too tightly) in rib (k above k, p above p). Sew or crochet armholes together from inside. Sew in or knot the ends.

Instructions

Family Beanie and Family Headband

Basic yarn ★ *Basic yarn 1 (main colour)* › 1 strand Peruvian Highland Wool alone. *Basic yarn 2 (pattern colour)* › 2 strands Tilia or 1 strand Arwetta plus 1 strand scrap yarn (Yarn types and alternatives, p. 254).

Scrap yarn ★ Varying lengths of thick, thin, smooth and shaggy yarns, wound to balls or skeins (p. 234). Or simply lots of balls or skeins of leftover yarns that you already have. The Family Beanie and Family Headband turn out best if you use only scrap yarn for needle size 3-4. That way the pattern won't come out wavy (which wouldn't look great on your head).

Size ★ 1 (2). Size 1 is good for kids but also for adults with a small to medium head (like me). Size 2 fits adults with a normal-sized head.

Measurement of garment ★ Approx. 47 (56) cm. Measure your head and choose a size that's a few centimetres smaller than your head.

Yarn requirement ★ *Basic yarn 1* › 2 balls Peruvian Highland Wool for both sizes. *Basic yarn 2* › 1 ball Tilia or 1 ball Arwetta for both sizes. Scrap yarn › At least 20 g.

If you want it to be a bobble hat, you will need 1 additional ball of basic yarn 1.

Needles ★ Circular needle size 5, 60 cm (for edge and top without pattern), dpn size 5 (for top of hat, if you are not knitting with Magic Loop, p. 239), circular needle size 4, 60 cm (for folded edge and pattern).

Tension square ★ Approx. 17 sts and 24-27 rows St st with needles size 5 = 10 x 10 cm. (Tension, p. 239). If your gauge is different, use thicker or thinner needles.

Colour chart C, p. 85.

I often think back to my holidays in Norway with my dad. He always loved the great outdoors because that's where he was in his element. And that was fantastic for me. This bobble hat is the epitome of a genuine Norwegian hat. "Bobble hat"! I looove that word, don't you?! But you can also make a headband – with the same instructions – but with a folded edge instead of ribbing because I think it looks amazing. The real pros with a PhD in knitting probably think casting off and then carrying on knitting is twice the work. That may be. But the edge just comes out SOOO beautiful, even if it does take a tiny bit more effort.

Knit the hat as long or short as you like. You can make it fit your head exactly, or knit it longer for a really cool 90s vibe. Once, when I was on holiday in Norway, I put a cheeseburger in my hat. It kept really nice and warm, I can tell you! To get the right length, try the hat on before you start decreasing and factor in an extra 5-8 cm of length for the decreases. A pompom or two will add the finishing touch (p. 99).

"Bobble hat"! I looove that word, don't you?!

Headband knitted in dark brown + scrap as the main colour and white as the pattern colour. To be honest, I made a mistake in this headband. I was watching something really exciting on telly (White Lotus 2) and forgot to count the rows. There shouldn't be quite so much white at the bottom. Oops.

Picking up stitches for the top of the hat.

Great! Also in the picture is my twenty-year-old Louis.

Basic instructions

Folded double-layer edge (headband) ★ Cast on 80 (96) sts with 1 strand basic yarn 1 and circular needle size 5. Place marker at beg of rnd = centre of back of headband/hat. Close to rnd and work 19 rnds in St st. Switch to circular needle size 4 (for folded edge and Fair Isle), p 1 rnd. Continue with needle size 4, working pattern in basic yarn 2 (don't forget to add the scrap!) as shown in colour chart (20 rnds in total). Now for the fold. This is the fun bit! With needle size 5 pick up 80 (96) sts along cast-on edge. Make sure you get exactly the right number stitches, otherwise the edge will come out crooked. Fold work over so that picked-up sts are on WS and work forms wide, flat tube with purl sides facing inwards. You now have 2 parallel circular needles with stitches. Each time you knit a st, knit 1 from front and 1 from back needle together, casting off as you go. Sew ends into inside of tube before closing it fully. If you are making the headband, stop here. Sit back and enjoy your evening off. If you are knitting the hat, move on to the next bit.

Top section of hat ★ With circular needle size 5, pick up 80 (96) sts from cast-off edge. Use sts right behind the cast-off sts so that the edge stands out nicely. Work 1st rnd in St st, placing 4 markers in total: at beg of rnd, after 20 (24) sts, after 40 (48) sts and after 60 (72) sts. You will need the markers for your decreases. I find it easiest to place the markers early. Then I can relax. Work in St st in rnds until hat is desired length – excluding crown. Factor in approx. 5-8 cm for crown. For a snug fit, you will need to knit between 5 and 9 cm, depending on size of head. If you prefer a cool 90s look, work approx. 10-15 cm. Crown and decreases › * k1, k2tog (p. 244), continue in St st until 3 sts remain before marker, SKP (p. 244), k1*. Slip marker from left to right needle, rep from * to * to end of rnd and in every second rnd. If using a circular needle, knit with Magic Loop (p. 239) for as long as you can. When it gets impossible, switch to dpn. (Personally, I find it impossible.) When 8 sts remain, cut off yarn and thread through remaining sts clockwise. Pull hard to close hole. Sew in or knot the ends.

Pompoms ★ Oooh, we did those in handicraft lessons at school! So, let's just pretend we're at school. Pompoms are awesome. But if you ask me, there are quite a lot of not-so-great pompoms around. Often they look at bit tatty, kind of measly and sad. For me, a good, mature pompom has two important things: lots and lots of yarn, and a carefully cut shape – a proper trim, in other words. Make the pompom in the size you think will go well with your hat. You might want a really big one. Or a medium-sized one. Or maybe even two? The diameter of the template will be the diameter of your pompom. I like pompoms to be 6-8 cm wide. 8 cm makes a huge pompom. Be warned!

There are all sorts of plastic gadgets around to help you make pompoms. If you're lucky enough to have the IQ needed to get how they work, then go ahead. I don't. I'm a fan of the good old cardboard circle.

Lifecycle of a pompom. That could be the title of my third book. Let's wait and see what Gyldendal says.

Here's how to make a pompom

- ★ Find an object (such as a cup or glass) to use as a template, with the diameter you want for your pompom. Place it on a piece of cardboard and draw round the edge. You will need to draw two identical circles. Then draw a smaller circle in the middle of each bigger circle. Cut out the circles so you end up with a donut shape.
- ★ Cut into the circles until you reach the middle hole. Then place the two circles on top of each other and wind yarn around them – in your main colour, for instance. Make sure you wrap the yarn evenly around the circle as it will pay off later, when you do the trim. If you want some coloured highlights, add in a little of your pattern yarn with scrap from time to time. It's going to look great! Maybe just use two or three different types of strand because less is more (sometimes, at least). Keep winding until the middle hole is completely full up – and don't be stingy with your yarn! When that's done, take a sharp pair of scissors and cut through the wound yarn all the way along the crack between the edges of the two cardboard circles.
- ★ Now insert a thread between the two cardboard circles and around the wrapped yarn in the middle. Pull it tight around the wrapped yarn and tie a knot. You will need to do this fairly quickly so that the cut strands of yarn don't fall out of place. The thread will then hold the yarn strands of the pompom together. You can also use it to attach the pompom to the hat. Pull off the cardboard circles. You can use them again.
- ★ Next, trim, trim and trim again until the pompom looks good. Cut carefully, a little at a time, so you can control the shape – but don't cut off too much. Trimming the pompom into shape will take a while, so enjoy the process and dream of the bobble hats you wore as a kid.
- ★ Steam the finished pompom, for instance over a pot of boiling water, or over the kettle while you are heating up water for a nice cup of coffee. That will fluff up the fibres nicely.

Barbie Knit

Family Sweater

Basic yarn ★ *Basic yarn 1 (main colour)* › 1 strand Peruvian Highland Wool. *Basic yarn 2 (pattern colour)* › 1 strand Tilia or 1 strand Arwetta or 1 strand Mille Colori Baby plus 1 strand scrap yarn (Yarn types and alternatives, p. 254).

Scrap yarn ★ Varying lengths of thick, thin, smooth or shaggy yarns etc., wound into balls or skeins (p. 234). Or just strands of leftover yarns. After all, you don't need much.

Size ★ One size.

Yarn requirement ★ At least 20 g.

Needles ★ Size 4 for ribbing, size 5 for the rest. (It's up to you whether you use circular or straight needles to knit in rows), dpn size 4 for rollneck, crochet hook size 4 for assembly.

Technique ★ Knit single star from colour chart B (p. 85) without the little sparkles in between. Colour chart for star is 13 sts by 13 rows.

Basic instructions

Front and back ★ Cast on 19 sts in basic yarn 1 on size 4 needles. Continue in rib (k1, p1). Work 2-4 rows for ribbing. Don't forget to BUTT. Switch to size 5 needles and continue in St st, p 1 round without pattern. *Next row (RS)* › BUTT, k2 (for border), work 13 sts in pattern (star only) as in colour chart, k3 (for border), turn. Continue in pattern with 3 sts of St st on both sides as border and BUTT for edge until complete. Work 3 rows without pattern. *Next row* › BUTT, k4, cast off middle 9 sts, k5. *Next row* › BUTT, p4, cast on 9 new sts (p. 244) for neck hole, continue across shoulder with p4, k1. Work 17 rows in St st without pattern with BUTT for edges. Switch to size 4 needles. Continue in rib as for front. Cast off.

Sleeve ★ Knit sleeves onto front and back as described on p. 138. Work 12 sts on size 5 needle, i.e. 6 sts on each side of shoulder seam. BUTT, p 1 row. *Next row* › BUTT, k 1 row. Continue until you have 12 rows of St st. Switch to size 4 needle. Work 4 rows in rib. Cast off. Knit second sleeve in exactly the same way.

Assembly ★ Close side and sleeve seams (p. 243). Knot the ends.

Fold-down rollneck ★ Using size 4 dpn, pick up 18 sts around neck hole. Work 12 rows in rib. Cast off and fold down rollneck.

I'm strong. But weak too.

On this one I was too busy watching telly again (Barnaby), so I made a mistake. I forgot the middle row on Barbie's pullover. What's also interesting to see is the difference between basic yarn + scrap used as the pattern colour (Ken) or the main colour (Barbie).

TUBORG

I love Liam

Chapter 3

Houndstooth, the big dream of playing the classy lady, and why we should always say good things before it's too late.

CHANEL
CHANEL

I tried so hard to stay cool, but my god was I disappointed and sad.
This wasn't about bags and scarves but about dreams and pathways through life.

I used to love playing "classy lady". That's what I used to call it – when I was a kid. We would try on clothes, pose in front of the mirror, take photos and then try on more clothes. It wasn't about being pretty or beautiful but about looking interesting or exciting. You can change your style and message, make up a story or be someone else but still be the same person – simply by changing your outfit! I love clothes, always have and always will. As if it was only classy ladies that loved clothes! As if…

By the time I was six or seven, I had designed my first collections. I even priced them. I was better at pricing then than now. Hats, dresses, tops, skirts, shoes – my collections were complete. I was obsessed with pretending to be a classy lady and being a fashion designer and stylist. I would spend hours trying on my mum's clothes and would mess up her entire wardrobe. I can still remember how amazing it felt to put on a satin bomber-jacket of hers with shoulder pads and a pair of pink carrot-fit trousers. Yay! I still rummage through her wardrobe now and she still doesn't like me messing everything up and forgetting to put things back. Sorry, but I'm not sorry, Mum. My daughter does exactly the same with my wardrobe, by the way.

When I was a kid, I used to collect fashion magazines – new and used ones. I rarely cut things out because I wanted them to remain intact. I was a collector and loved to look at them again and again. The runway photos were the most exciting. I would dream of patterns, feel, textiles and silhouettes before I even knew the words for them. I also read the small print every time: who designed what? What was the model called? Who did the styling? Who was the make-up artist? And the editor? By the time I was twelve I knew all the names in fashion in Paris and Copenhagen. Since then, I have actually got to meet a number of them as well, through my work. And I have to admit, I'm not very good at staying cool. I was born a fan-girl and will always be one.

I also used to make my own fashion magazines by cutting stuff out, editing it and also writing my own copy – I had an opinion on clothes – and still do. And the heaps of fashion magazines that mustn't have anything cut out of them have grown exponentially.

SHOP

zebre
Støvler fra kenzo
Støvler fra Gucci
Julens Nyemode
enmasse nye frisurer
nr.2
20,000
350
1000
800
15,000
ADIDAS
ADI das

LOL
I was much better at pricing my designs when I was a kid!
t-shirt fra Chanel
EXIT
MODE MODE
kæde
top
bukser
Kjole
15.000
Hat
500

My greatest wish at age 11 was to have a silk scarf from one of the big French fashion houses. Sounds crazy, I know, and it was completely unnecessary, superfluous and useless. Especially for an 11-year-old. But somehow it wasn't: that silk scarf was a dream of mine. To me it was an iconic designer piece, a symbol, and a little piece of the world I found so infinitely fascinating. I was almost obsessed. All I could think of was to hold this scarf in my hand, to feel it, to own it. If only I had that scarf, I would be a little bit closer to my dream, and my dream wouldn't be out of reach.

But where I was, there weren't any shops that sold that type of scarf. I had only seen it in magazines. One day, when we were planning a summer holiday in France, my mum told me they had all the shops I had been dreaming of so passionately there. The boutiques I had only read and heard about. So I saved up for a whole year, doing cleaning jobs, collecting returnable bottles, asking for money for my birthday, working in the garden and so on.

Finally, the day came when I was able to spend my savings. Nervous and excited, I pulled on my smartest gear: Airwalks and an orange-and-brown polo shirt. We walked into the extremely high-end boutique and found the sales assistant was neither particularly nice nor especially helpful. But my mother insisted they serve me. The sales assistant showed me the most beautiful scarf, and in my school English I stammered: "How much?" The sales assistant told me the price. It was more than double what I had saved! I immediately burst into tears, sobbing my heart out. It had never even occurred to me that, despite all my efforts, having saved as hard as I could and really given my all, I still might not have enough money...

The sales assistant tried to console me, in French, and gave me a free catalogue. It was a thick, hard-cover book with photos of the 1997 collection. I was thrilled to bits. As I stepped out of the shop, Henning, my wonderful stepdad, was standing there ready with his camera and took a photo of me trying to hold back my tears and not look utterly devastated. After that disappointment, I grew even more adamant in my wish to possess a tiny piece of that world. And probably to have the right to determine my own future as well. I still have the catalogue and will never forget the experience. And I spent the whole journey there and back, across Europe, knitting.

Oh yes, and then there was our school trip to Paris too! On that trip I spent everything I had earned (from my two jobs, working four days a week) and my entire savings for a pair of Marc Jacobs stilettos. I also ate and drank nothing but my classmates' leftovers. I couldn't even afford to send my mum a postcard. I think she was a bit upset. But at least I brought a pair of stilettos home with me. Luckily, I have come to my senses a bit since then. Only a tiny bit, though.

Don't let things get you down!

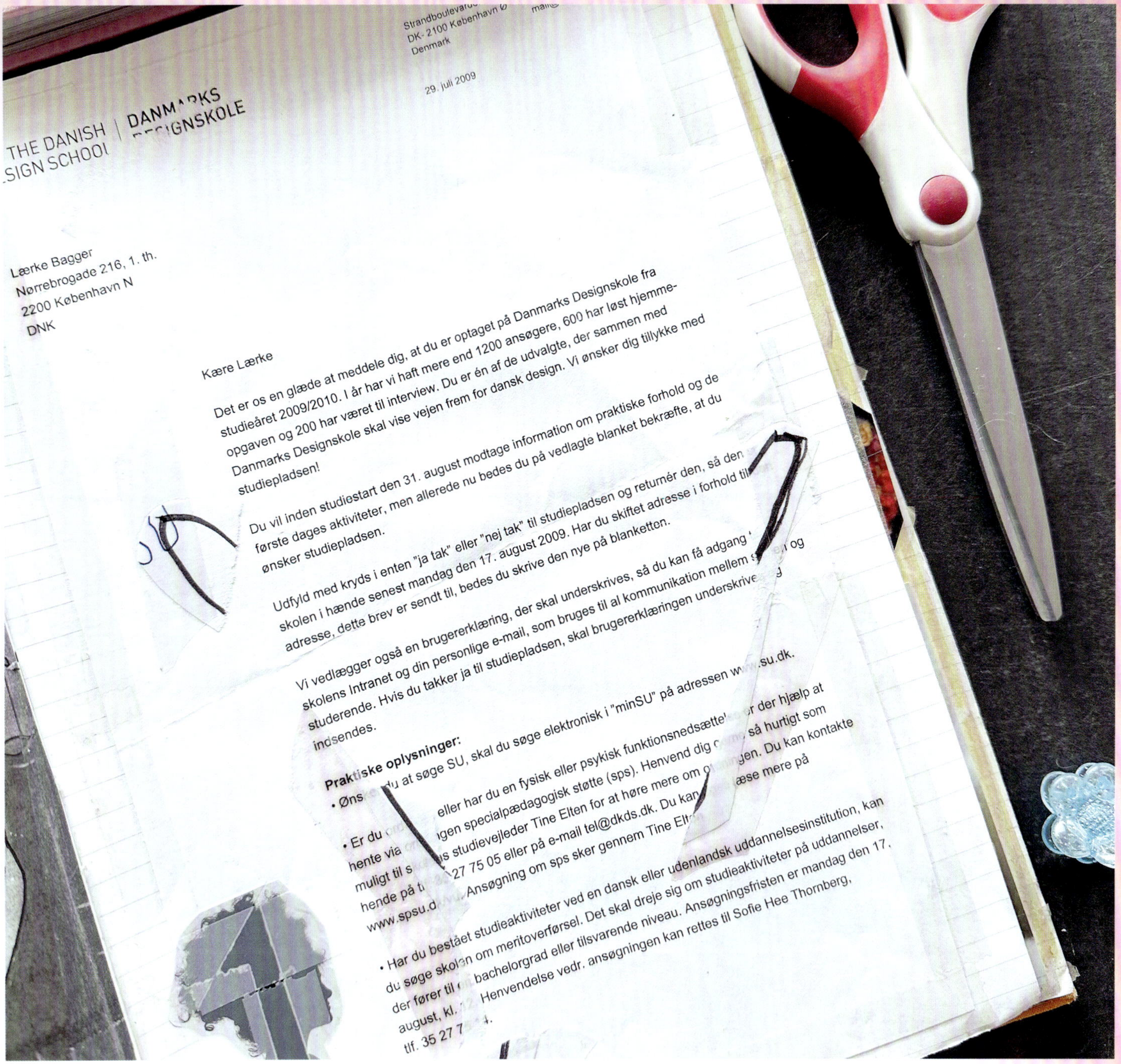
Strandboulevard
DK-2100 København Ø
Denmark

29. juli 2009

THE DANISH DESIGN SCHOOL | DANMARKS DESIGNSKOLE

Lærke Bagger
Nørrebrogade 216, 1. th.
2200 København N
DNK

Kære Lærke

Det er os en glæde at meddele dig, at du er optaget på Danmarks Designskole fra studieåret 2009/2010. I år har vi haft mere end 1200 ansøgere, 600 har løst hjemme-opgaven og 200 har været til interview. Du er én af de udvalgte, der sammen med Danmarks Designskole skal vise vejen frem for dansk design. Vi ønsker dig tillykke med studiepladsen!

Du vil inden studiestart den 31. august modtage information om praktiske forhold og de første dages aktiviteter, men allerede nu bedes du på vedlagte blanket bekræfte, at du ønsker studiepladsen.

Udfyld med kryds i enten "ja tak" eller "nej tak" til studiepladsen og returnér den, så den skolen i hænde senest mandag den 17. august 2009. Har du skiftet adresse i forhold til adresse, dette brev er sendt til, bedes du skrive den nye på blanketten.

Vi vedlægger også en brugererklæring, der skal underskrives, så du kan få adgang skolens Intranet og din personlige e-mail, som bruges til al kommunikation mellem og studerende. Hvis du takker ja til studiepladsen, skal brugererklæringen underskrives indsendes.

Praktiske oplysninger:

- Har du bestået studieaktiviteter ved en dansk eller udenlandsk uddannelsesinstitution, kan du søge skolen om meritoverførsel. Det skal dreje sig om studieaktiviteter på uddannelser, der fører til bachelorgrad eller tilsvarende niveau. Ansøgningsfristen er mandag den 17. august, kl. Henvendelse vedr. ansøgningen kan rettes til Sofie Hee Thornberg, tlf. 35 27 7

"You are admitted to the Danish School of Design in the academic year 2009/2010..."

My love of clothes and fashion has not faded over the years either, and the more I learned about handicrafts, the more I had the urge to create clothes. I was still young when I told a careers adviser I wanted to be a fashion designer. He advised me to study something easier. Cool.

I don't remember if I ever told my dad about my dream of being accepted into design school. I guess not. I was probably too scared and reluctant to risk being laughed at or having to justify myself to someone who never justified anything he did. And he had often told me what he thought of clothes and aesthetics. He was super-critical.

By the way, if you have a dream of something that seems impossible, let me tell you: nothing is impossible. But it will definitely be impossible if you don't try.

But I was lucky and good enough to get a place at the school. When I got my letter of admission, I cried. I still have the letter today. My dad totally didn't get why I wanted to go there or what I was going to do. And he never tired of telling me so. As for me, I was so proud to have been accepted into the School of Design at the Art Academy that I still can't even describe the feeling properly: I was about to explode, totally over the moon because I had finally found something I felt I had always been looking for. I was on the path I had always dreamed of. By the way, if you have a dream of something that seems impossible, let me tell you: nothing is impossible. But it will be impossible if you don't try.

By the time I started at Design School, my father had already been living in Greenland for seven years. The only contact we had was a few letters and emails every year. He was very much stuck in his world there, and that was all he wrote about. And I was stuck in mine: Design School, friends, and the occasional big draft beer – plus all my yarns, knitting and fashion.

Although my dad and I wrote about our lives, I didn't get the sense he really read and understood what I was saying. And to be honest, I didn't read his stories about his world properly either. I read them – but not properly. We were just too far apart. There was too much distance between us, both physically and mentally. He pointed it out himself, very directly, by signing all his emails "Får" (sheep) instead of "Far" (dad). At first I thought it was a mistake and I had misread his handwriting. But over time, I realised it was a comment on our relationship.

That really upset me. But now I realise he was probably just making a bad joke about himself. The "sheep" was a kind of self-preservation and a way to refer to himself that made him less vulnerable. Our relationship was fraught with misunderstandings. What a massive waste of precious time. He called me Laaki, by the way, which is Greenlandic for Lærke.

A few years before he died, my dad bought himself a house in northern Jutland. He wanted to come back to Denmark – eventually. I was really excited when he wrote that. Finally there was light at the end of the tunnel! The house gave me hope that more was to come. It was a little declaration of love and reconciliation. But my dad never made it back here and I never got to visit him in his house. The first time I saw it was on the day of his funeral – it's 20 metres from his grave.

After my dad died, it was my job to clear out his house. But I just couldn't bear to. It was too hard. So, I did the whole thing in two days and checked the contents of as many of his 60 removal boxes as I could. They contained his entire life, which I had never really been a part of and which I didn't know or understand. There was a deathly silence in the house, and yet it felt as though everything was screaming at me, telling me I had been a terrible daughter, a failure, that it was my fault everything had gone so wrong between us, that I hadn't done enough and that now, it was too late. I still have a few of his boxes in my basement, but I have not yet had the courage to look inside them. They contain letters that he wrote to me but never sent. Imagine if they were full of terrible things! Or, even worse, if they were full of lovely messages that never got to me...

In his bedroom I found a whole drawer full of cuttings from newspapers and magazines that were about me. All those years he had bought, collected and read all these things – but never told me about it. Nor did he ever say he was interested in my knitting or proud of me. Why didn't he say so? Over his bed hung two pictures: one of John Lennon and one of me. Just think of all that meaningless chatter we could have saved ourselves. All those empty words about fresh seal fat and half-fisherman's rib in untreated wool. That day, in his house in north Jutland, I made a decision: never to bottle up care, praise, love or admiration inside me. What a waste! If you have something good to say, say it. Always. Starting today. Pay someone a compliment. Don't keep it to yourself – get it out there. Because it could benefit, delight, change or encourage them.

I have created a design that reminds me of everything I think my dad didn't accept or understand about me: all the cheerfulness and positivity I love about myself. Which he also loved. But which I thought he *didn't* love. So, let's just be nice to people all the time – without guilt or shame – because we really have no time to lose.

This is the very first *Fancy Sweater* I ever knitted. With raglan sleeves. Never again! Keeping four repeats going all at the same time is tricky, especially while watching telly (Gilmore Girls). Take a look at page 132 instead. There's a better, updated version of the design there.

That day, in his house in north Jutland,
I made a decision: never to bottle up care, praise,
love or admiration inside me. What a waste!
If you have something good to say, say it. Always.
Starting today. Pay someone a compliment.
Don't keep it to yourself – get it out there. Because
it could benefit, delight, change or
encourage them.

My first process book, from 1996.
And the first (and last) shoes I designed
around that time in crafting lessons.
Platform slide wedges made of wood
with a leather soul and leather upper.
Miuccia, just give me a call!

Matching: *Fancy Cardy* (p. 132) and *Fancy Tube Top* (p. 142) with awesome buttons.

Houndstooth – a bit about the pattern

Houndstooth is one of the most famous textile patterns in the world. It's absolutely brilliant and instantly recognisable. And it's easy and great fun to knit too because the repeat is not too long. And, of course, it's beautiful. For more on Fair Isle knitting with multiple strands, see p 77. The same technique is used here.

Houndstooth is knitted with two different-coloured yarns. Let's call them main colour and pattern colour, as before, because that makes it easier to explain. Choose a basic yarn as your main colour and another basic yarn as your pattern colour. Ideally, the two shades should contrast nicely because that's how it looks best. You then knit an additional strand of scrap yarn in, with either your main or your pattern colour.

How the pattern turns out depends on which yarn is the dominant one (Pattern dominance, p. 82). It's up to you whether you want the main or pattern colour to dominate. Just try a few things out, knit a few swatches and remember: it's always good to work with contrasts in Fair Isle knitting because contrasts make the pattern stand out.

You can also knit different-coloured stripes, of course, in your pattern colour as well as your main colour – that looks really great!

Fancy Bag (p. 126) before felting.

Fancy Bag (p. 126) after felting.

A huge stack of *Fancy Bags* (p. 126), all individually felted – because washing machines are like people: no two are the same.

To felt or not to felt?

For years I thought felting was tacky, overkill, old-fashioned. But in actual fact it was me that was tacky, overkill, old-fashioned. Felt is hot, hot, hot!

A few years ago, I was sitting in the legendary Bodega Vintsue 90, having a few beers with my friend from Design School. Next to us was a woman in the most amazing felt jacket. My friend and I – who are both textile freaks – spent ages talking about how we had never seen such beautiful felt. We decided to compliment the woman on her choice of outfit. It turned out she was Jytte Hilden, former Minister of Culture in Denmark. Needless to say, we struck up a conversation. Afterwards, talking about our chance encounter with the former Culture Minister over a beer in a bodega, my friend, who is American, said "Only in Denmark". And she is not the only minister I have bumped into in a pub!

When you felt wool, the combination of water, heat and rubbing causes the fibres to become matted, creating a tough, thick material. You will need to use yarn that can be felted, of course – pure, untreated wool, in other words, not superwash. If in doubt, ask at the wool shop. I have often done that.

Have you ever felted before? If you have, you will know that the easiest way of doing it is in the washing machine. You can do it by hand as well, but quite frankly, who would do that if they were making a great big bag out of thick wool? Anyway, the official instruction for felting with a machine is: 30-40 degrees in a standard programme without prewash and with normal spinning. That's all you need. My official instruction is: knit a small tension square with the right needle size and the right yarn (wait, did she say tension square???), stick it in the washing machine and test it at 30 degrees. All the washing machines I've seen do different things, and I have ruined a lot of things by over-felting them. If 30 degrees doesn't work, try 40.

By the way, everyone I talk to about felting says it's definitely easiest to do in a dryer. (And very time-saving too.) It takes about 10-15 minutes, but you need to keep an eye on what's going on the whole time. That's all well and good, of course, but it assumes that you do actually have the completely absurd luxury of a tumble dryer. Not everyone is so lucky. But I am hereby passing the advice on to you, and you can follow it if you like. At your own risk, of course.

All you do is felt your item in the same machine as you are washing your clothes in anyway. Not with your very best outfit, of course, just to be on the safe side. And nor should you felt your knits with other wool clothes in the machine, or else you might suddenly end up with a massive lump of unusable wool. Towels, for example, are perfectly suited, so throw a few of those in the drum, as they will increase the friction and boost the felting effect. And don't forget to put in some detergent!

When you have dragged the monster out of the machine, simply pull it into shape while it's damp. If the handle of the bag has turned out too short from the felting, for instance, just give it a pull. In other words, if the sight of your knit emerging from the machine is enough to make you want to throw up, don't panic. I have this really great technique that involves standing on the bag while I pull the handle. It works a treat!

While your felted item is drying, you will need to be patient, as it can take days. Turn it inside out from time to time – and then back again after a while. That way both sides will dry nicely, and your funky bag won't start to pong.

You can felt all sorts of things: football boots, hats, clutches, mittens – you name it.

Also, if you felt your knits, you can't see the mistakes so much. WIN!

If you have anything good to say, then say it.

Scrap yarn and felting – Dos and don'ts

If you want to felt something, it's best to make it from wool that can be felted. HOWEVEEERRR, I wouldn't be Lærke Bagger if I stuck to the rules, would I? So, me being me, I had to try out what would happen if I mixed random types of felting wool with my scrap yarns. And it came out absolutely great! My conclusion is highly satisfying: if you use a feltable yarn as your basic yarn, you can easily knit a strand of scrap yarn in with it. Because if some of the strands are felted and others aren't, it looks absolutely awesome! Don't worry, the strands will still all be together even after they have been through the washing machine. If you don't believe me, try it out yourself!

Needless to say, I have saved the best till last. If you use scrap yarn to felt with, a single knot is all you need to attach it because it will come out felted anyway. YAY! And nor do you need to cut the ends off. Cool! If you don't like the ends, just cut them off when your knitted item has been felted and had time to dry.

I have got into the habit of saving even the tiniest, most impractical ends of thread and tying them together to make a big ball of wool – from which I then knitted a felt bag.

Instructions

Fancy Bag

Basic yarn ★ Peruvian Highland Wool or Fritidsgarn. The number of strands you use depends on which bag you are making (Yarn types and alternatives, p. 254).

Scrap yarn ★ Varying lengths of thick, thin, smooth and shaggy yarns, wound to balls or skeins (p. 234). Or simply lots of balls or skeins of leftover yarns that you already have.

Size ★ 1 (2). Size 1 is a handbag. Size 2 is a shopping bag. All three versions come in two sizes.

The three versions of the Fancy Bag
Small bag ★ (Base › needle size 5, 60 cm, rest of bag needle size 8, 60 cm). Can be made with e.g. 1 strand Peruvian Highland Wool plus 1 strand scrap yarn as main colour, and 2 strands Peruvian Highland Wool (as pattern colour).

Medium bag ★ (Base › needle size 7, 60 cm, rest of bag needle size 10, 80 cm). Can be made with e.g. 2 strands Peruvian Highland Wool plus 1 strand scrap yarn (as main colour) and 3 strands Peruvian Highland Wool (as pattern colour); or 1 strand Fritidsgarn plus 1 strand scrap yarn (as main colour) and 2 strands Fritidsgarn (as pattern colour).

Large bag ★ (Base › needle size 9, 60 cm, rest of bag needle size 12, 80 cm). Can be made with e.g. 3 strands Peruvian Highland Wool plus 1 strand scrap yarn (as main colour) and 4 strands Peruvian Highland Wool (as pattern colour); or 2 strands Fritidsgarn plus 1 strand scrap yarn (as main colour) and 3 strands Fritidsgarn (as pattern colour).

Yarn requirement
Small bag ★ At least 2 balls Peruvian Highland Wool (as main colour) + at least 2 balls Peruvian Highland Wool (as pattern colour). At least 30 g scrap yarn.

Medium bag ★ At least 3 balls Peruvian Highland Wool or Fritidsgarn (as main colour) + at least 3 balls Peruvian Highland Wool or Fritidsgarn (as pattern colour). At least 40 g scrap yarn.

Large bag ★ At least 6 balls Peruvian Highland Wool or Fritidsgarn (as main colour) + at least 6 balls Peruvian Highland Wool or Fritidsgarn (as pattern colour). At least 50 g scrap yarn.

Needles ★ Depend on which version you are making.

Tension square ★ No comment. Not important. All the bags I have seen were different sizes and tensions but always totally awesome. Felting in the washing machine, needle thicknesses and Fair Isle all affect the result, as do scrap yarns and basic yarns. But fun is guaranteed.

Colour chart D, p. 129.

>

Cheesy Wotsits or cheese croissants????

A size 1 small bag and a size 1 large bag. Plus my cool outdoor crocs, which I paid for myself.

Fancy Bag in ombre (replace one strand every 4th or 5th row/round until all the strands have been replaced. Shown here in black to dark brown.

White + scrap as the main colour, red + black as the pattern colour.

A truly snazzy bag – Lærke Bagger style. I love bags. Any bags. Cheap, expensive, plastic, fabric, nice, practical or even completely useless bags. Basically, I love any kind of container you can stuff all your odds and ends into. The more the merrier. The *Fancy Bag* is my proposal for a design that's a mixture of everything. It comes in two sizes: handbag size and shopper size. Maybe you don't want to take too much stuff with you? Or maybe you want a bag you can fit loaaads of stuff into?

You can also make the bag in any of three different variants, in different yarns and with different needle sizes, depending on the version you want to make. The different variants cover needle sizes 8-12 mm – so there should be something for everyone. If you don't like knitting with a 12, just knit the medium-sized or smaller version. If it's sounding confusing, look at the pictures.

You can knit the bag with or without at pattern. And of course in 1000 variations that you get to choose yourself. Confused? Stressed? Don't be! Because this bag is such fun to knit that you will end up with more and more ideas popping up all the time. As you will see when you try it out.

You will need two colours: a main colour and a pattern colour. The main colour is for making the base and handle. Personally, I like to combine main colours with scrap yarn, but you do it your way. If you can't be bothered with a pattern or 10,000 different yarns and balls, just make the bag in unicolour. That looks great too! When you have finished knitting, the bag will look huge and hideous. But that's because – tadaaah! – it needs to go in the washing machine to be felted, baby. Don't worry. But before you go any further, take a look at p. 123 and read up on the basics of felting. There are no measurements provided for these bags, by the way, because they all come out differently once they are felted anyway.

Basic instructions

Base of bag ★ The base consists of a rectangle in stocking stitch. You then pick up stitches along the edges of the base to create the sides of the bag. Using your chosen yarn and the right number of strands as specified for the bag-size and version you are knitting, cast on 10 (15) sts in your main colour – using two needles... you know... like grandma does. If you cast on this way, it's easier to pick up stitches from the edge later because the casting on is not so tight. Knit rows in St st. Don't forget to BUTT (p. 242) the edges. The BUTT is important because it makes it easier to pick up stitches later and creates a neater join. Work 40 (60) rows in total. Cast off loosely.

Picking up sts ★ From the edges of the rectangular base, pick up 60 (90) sts with the same needle and yarn (main colour). This will give you the same number of sts as there are sts and rows in base, if you followed the instructions and did BUTTs at the edges. Pick up the stitches through the outer loops of the sts and rows so that the base and sides of the bag join neatly. Starting in the middle of a narrow side, mark beg of rnd = side of bag. On each narrow side (cast-on and cast-off edges of base) pick up 10 (15) sts. On the long sides pick up 20 (30) sts (Size 1 › 10 + 20 + 10 + 20 = 60 sts. Size 2 › 15 + 30 + 15 + 30 = 90 sts). Pick up 30 (45) sts (= one half of bag), then place marker (= other half of bag). Keep moving your markers up as you work – you will need them to knit the handle. Pick up another 30 (45) sts. You are now back at your first marker and at beg of rnd (= 60 (90) picked-up sts). Close to form rnd.
Next rnd › Depending on which version you are making, switch to bigger needles and work 1 rnd. After every 3 sts inc 1 = *k3, inc 1*, rep from * to * to end of rnd. I find it easiest to inc through back loop of k st (p. 244). You now have 80 (120) sts and are totally ready for the Fair Isle bit (or to continue in unicolour).

Patterned (or unicolour) section ★ Using your chosen yarn and the right number of strands, work pattern as in colour chart D. Make sure you don't pull your floats too tight (p. 78) or the pattern will come out distorted and your bag won't look even. It will look ugly when felted. So, it's best to knit sloppily and loosely, even if it does make your hair stand on end.

Place a marker in the middle of each of the narrow sides of the base. See hearts.

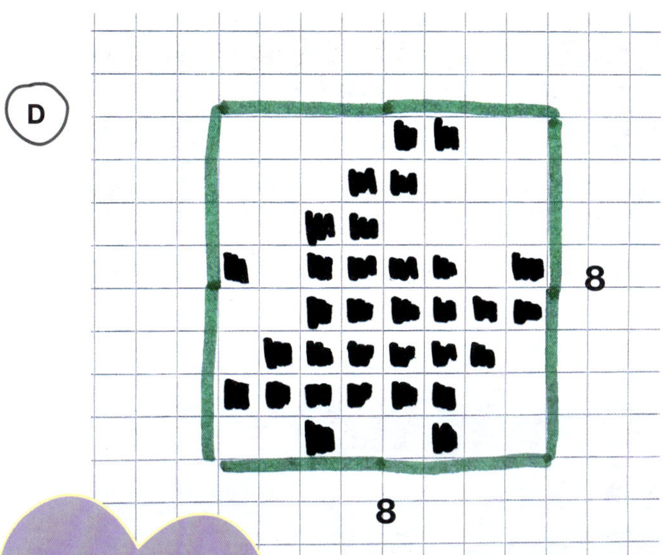

Applies to all three Fancy instructions (p. 126, 132, 142).

>

H: 20cm
B: 25cm

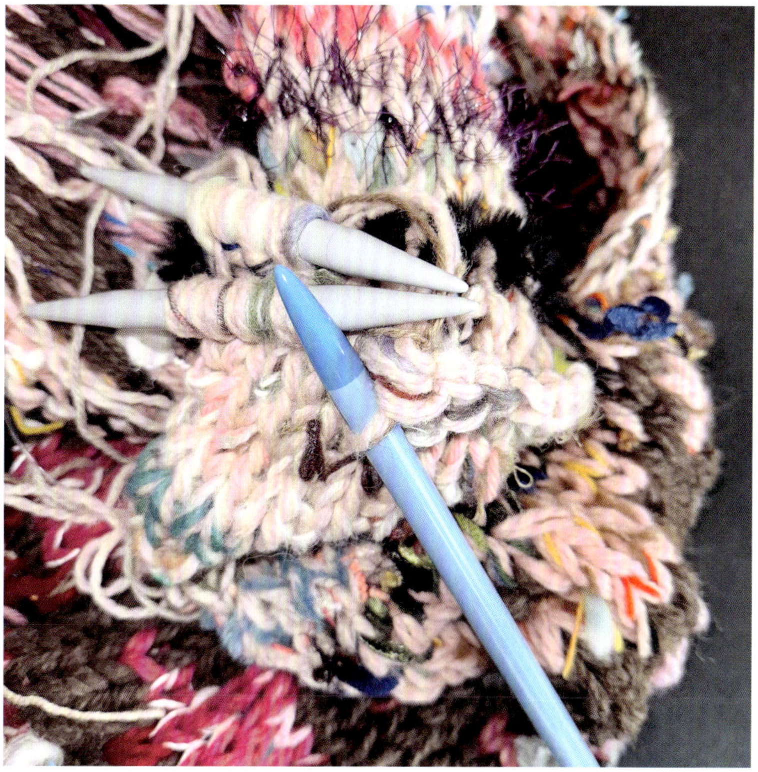

Here's how to knit the two parts of the handle together.

Stay cool. It's going to be felted, remember? Continue pattern as in colour chart to end of rnd and rep 3 (4) times up bag. Unicolour: Work 24 (32) rnds. Pattern: Cut off pattern-colour yarn and work 1 rnd in yarn used for base (main colour). Now decrease for top of bag. Next rnd › *k1, k2tog (p. 244), continue in St st until 3 sts remain before marker, SKP (p. 244), k1*. Slip marker from left to right needle, rep from * to * to end of rnd = 4 sts dec, 76 (116) sts remaining. Next rnd › *Work 8 sts St st, cast off 22 (42) sts – tightly! (I know, I know, but when it's felted it'll look great), work 8 sts St st, slip marker from left to right needle, rep from * to end of rnd = 16 sts remaining on each side for the two handles.

Handles ★ Knit two handles. Handles are knitted separately in St st and joined by knitting them together at the end. It's easy. I just carry on knitting on the same circular needle while ignoring the other handle. But you might like to knit the handle on a different needle to make it easier to move. It's entirely up to you. Whatever you choose, the handles are made as follows: You are now at beg of rnd. (Leave marker on needle for the moment as it tells you where the middle of the handle is.) k8, turn, BUTT (p. 242), p14 to last st, k1 (for BUTT, of course). Next row (RS) › BUTT, *k1, k2tog, k1, SKP, k1*, slip marker from left to right needle, rep from * to * to end of row, k1. Turn, p to end of row (don't forget to BUTT the edge), now remove marker as it's no longer needed. *Next row (RS)* › BUTT, k1, k2tog, k to last 4 sts, SKP, k1, k1 for edge. *Next row (WS) and all WS rows* › BUTT, p to last st, k1 (for edge) = 10 sts remaining. Continue in St st until handle is desired length. You may like to mark 1st row after WS row as it will make it easier to count. I prefer a shortish handle that's still long enough to carry the bag on my shoulder. That's about 12 rows. But knit the handle as long as you like. You might want to make a crossbody bag that hangs at hip level or just under the top of your arm. End with WS row. Leave sts and move on to second handle. Cut off yarn. Start second handle on WS, BUTT (for edge), p14 to last st, k1 (for BUTT). Work decs as for first handle.

Knitting handles together ★ Lay the 2 needles with 10 sts each parallel and use a third (the same size) to knit sts from front and back needles together, casting off as you go. Cut off ends and knot them if needed. The bag is going to be felted, which will also felt the ends = sewing them in is a waste of time. Don't trim anything until after you have felted the bag – because then it will look quite different! Don't cut the ends off too short. You can always cut them shorter later. It's up to you how "crazy" you want the bag to look and how many ends you want dangling down – or not. But definitely felt it before you decide. Enjoy your life while you have it. After all, everything is a process.

Instructions

Fancy Cardy/Sweater

One Sunday I was sitting in the workshop with Lulu and putting fringes on this *Fancy Cardy*, when I noticed she was drawing my knitting.

Basic yarn ★ *Basic yarn 1 (main colour)* › 1 strand Fritidsgarn alone, or 1 strand Peruvian Highland Wool plus 1 strand Tilia or Arwetta. *Basic yarn 2 (pattern colour)* › 1 strand Fritidsgarn alone, or 3 strands Tilia, or 1 strand Peruvian Highland Wool plus 1 strand scrap yarn (Yarn types and alternatives, p. 254).

Scrap yarn ★ Varying lengths of thick, thin, smooth and shaggy yarns, wound to balls or skeins (p. 234). Or simply lots of balls or skeins of leftover yarns that you can knit stripes with.

Size ★ 1 (2) 3 (4) 5 (6) 7 (8) (Size guide, p. 239).

Chest measurement of garment ★ Approx. 104 (110) 129 (135) 153 (160) 178 (184) cm. This measurement is the total circumference measured just under the armhole.

Total length ★ Unfortunately it's impossible to say, as there are so many variations you can knit. But if you are knitting with the specified tension, one pattern repeat will be about 6 cm long. Plus the ribbing. For a short, very short or longer version of the knit, shorten/lengthen the front(s) and back before the armhole (Length, p. 250).

Yarn requirement ★ *Basic yarn 1* › At least 5 balls Fritidsgarn or Peruvian Highland Wool and at least 3 balls Tilia. *Basic yarn 2* › At least 4 balls Fritidsgarn, or at least 3 balls Tilia, or at least 4 balls Peruvian Highland Wool. *Scrap yarn* › At least 100 g.

Needles ★ Circular needle size 7, 80 cm (for sleeves, front(s) and back), circular needle size 6, 60-80 cm (for ribbing), crochet hook size 6 (for assembly).

Tension square ★ Approx. 13 sts and 12-14 rows of pattern on needle size 7 = 10 x 10 cm (Tension, p. 239) If your gauge is different, use thicker or thinner needles.

Colour chart D, p. 129.

I have been dressing up, making myself look really chic, trying on clothes, trying out outfits, trying to be someone else and be more myself – or whatever you call it – for as long as I can remember. The *Fancy Cardy/Sweater* is a homage to all kids and grown-ups who love(d) to play. It is an oversize fit inspired by the big shoulders of the 80s and 90s. I remember my mum had a pullover with that kind of silhouette, which I absolutely loved. The chest measurement may sound extreme, but remember: the front and back drop down over the shoulders too. If you want it tighter, knit a size smaller. But watch out for the chest measurement nonetheless.

The *Fancy Cardy/Sweater* is knitted in rows, with purls knitted according to the pattern. Whaaat? You know, knitting it in rows is definitely better than battling your way through four different repeats while doing raglan decreases. I know what I am talking about. I have tried both.

You can vary the design ad infinitum. Short sweater, long sweater, sweater dress, cardy, jacket, dressing gown, maybe even with shoulder pads (p. 271)? Or with some fringes on the edging, perhaps (p. 214)? Or maybe even an entire set with a bag and tube top? But remember: if you are making a long sweater or coat, knit it 5-8 cm shorter than the final length you want it to be. Long knits are heavy, so they almost always drop and get longer and longer as you wear them.

>

You can vary the design ad infinitum.

An extra-long *Fancy Cardy* in brown with an ombre effect in various red and pink mohair yarns. Start with the darkest colour and replace one strand of it with a lighter colour every four rows, until all the strands are the new colour. Keep going for as long as you like.

These patterns have a lot of writing. Because I'm being thorough. Purely for your benefit, of course. I would also like to say right now that all of the items shown here are knitted by me and contain at least three to five (major) mistakes. And you know what? I don't think anyone will even notice. Go ahead, try and find the five mistakes! Shhh... I'll tell you one of my big ones, OK? I hope my grandma isn't looking down from above while I say this... When I was picking up stitches for the sleeves, I forgot to turn the pattern "around" in my head. I did that with ALL five of these pullovers that I knitted, in fact. And you know what? You can't even see it. So why make life more difficult than it already is? Turn the pattern around if you want to. And if you don't, then don't. By "turning it around" I mean turning it upside down (which you can do quite simply by turning this book on its head). Then follow the colour chart so that the pattern on the sleeves matches the pattern on the front and back. By the way, I didn't "lock" the floats on the back of these. I think the front looks nicer if you don't lock them even though they extend across six stitches. And it's not necessary either (p. 78).

The *Fancy Cardy/Sweater* comes out nicest if you give it a gentle iron when you have finished (p. 250). Also, don't forget the edge stitches (e.g. BUTT, p. 242) because that way it's a LOT easier to assemble. And hey, don't worry about knitting Fair Isle from the back. Surely you're not scared of that, are you? By the way, I knitted the main and pattern colour strands into the last edge stitch (k1) in every row because it makes it easier to "pull" the strand along as you go (p. 80).

Basic instructions

Back (sweater and cardy) ★ Cast on 68 (72) 84 (88) 100 (104) 116 (120) sts on size 6 needle. Maybe you are knitting the same main colour throughout. Or maybe you are knitting it in stripes in different colours. Who knows? Either way › *BUTT 1st st, then work in rib (k1 tbl, p1) in rows until 1 st remains, k1. Turn. BUTT, continue in rib until until 1 st remains, k1*. Rep from * to * until ribbing is desired length. For a short version, that will be about 5 cm. For a long one, I think more ribbing looks best, about 11-12 cm. But make sure you knit an even number of rows so that your 2 rows of rib work out. Next row = RS row. Switch to needle size 7. *Work edge stitch on RS and WS rows all the way up the garment* › BUTT the first st, k last st. k1 (3) 1 (3) 1 (3) 1 (3). Start at beg of pattern repeat. Start with pattern colour and work as in colour chart until 2 (4) 2 (4) 2 (4) 2 (4) sts remain. k last sts (final st is edge st) Turn. *WS row* › BUTT, p1 (3) 1 (3) 1 (3) 1 (3). Continue in p as in colour chart until 2 (4) 2 (4) 2 (4) 2 (4) sts remain. p1 (3) 1 (3) 1 (3) 1 (3), end with k1 (edge st). Rep last 2 rows until back is desired length. Last row of pattern repeat is a WS row. *Next row* › Cut off pattern colour and cast off all sts knitwise in main colour. Put work aside.

Front with V-neck (sweater) ★ Front and back must be same length, i.e. with same length of ribbing and same number of pattern repeats. *That means* › Work front in exactly the same way as back until you get to the neck.

Basically, it's up to you how deep the V-neck will be. 1 recommend starting the shaping between 4 and 6 pattern repeats from the top: 4 for a higher neck, 5 for a medium one and 6 for a lower V-neck. Wait! What I mean is, start the V-neck when there are 4-6 pattern repeats less on the front than the back.

Arrange it so that you can start the pattern repeat on RS row and with the pattern facing you. Continue in pattern but don't forget to account for sts cast off along neck edge. So, where you continue on the colour chart will depend on how many sts you have cast off. This applies to rest of front and neck. It's easier than it sounds: the pattern repeat is just 8 sts high and 8 sts across, and you are familiar with it by now because you have done it all over the back and halfway up the front as well.

PERFECT

Black as the main colour and pale brown + scrap as the pattern colour.

Lilac as the main colour and pink + scrap as the pattern colour.

V-neck (sweater) ★ Work 33 (35) 41 (43) 49 (51) 57 (59) sts incl. edge st in pattern, cast off middle 2 sts (mark both sts), work remaining 33 (35) 41 (43) 49 (51) 57 (59) incl. edge st in pattern. Complete each side of neck separately. Start with left side of front, the "active" side. *Work edge st and pattern in WS row to last 2 sts. Include 1st of the 2 sts into edge st by purling it in main colour, k last st in main colour as well. Next row (RS) › BUTT, SKP (p. 244) in main colour, continue in pattern, work edge as before*. Rep from * to * until front with neck is same length and has same number of pattern repeats as back. Cast off on RS in main colour.

Work right side of neck in same way but in reverse. Start on WS row › *BUTT, p1 in main colour (include st in edge), work pattern in p, work edge st as before. Turn. Continue on RS. Work edge st and pattern as before until 3 sts remain, k2tog (p. 244) in main colour, k last st (edge)*. Rep last 2 rows from * to * until front and V-neck are same length on both sides and have same number of pattern repeats as back. Cast off on RS in main colour.

Fronts (cardy) ★ Start with right front. Back and fronts must be same length, i.e. with same length of ribbing and same number of pattern repeats. Cast on 41 (43) 49 (51) 57 (59) 65 (67) in main colour on needle size 6, BUTT, continue in rib (k1 tbl, p1) in rows until last st, k1. Turn. BUTT, continue in rib (p1 tbl, k1) to last st, k1. Rep these two rows until ribbing is desired length. End with WS row. Now knit pattern and button band at same time. I knit button bands straight onto the front to save all the faffing at the end. That way, it's just done. Switch to needle size 7. The button band is knitted over the 1st 6 sts on right front (and over last 6 sts on left front). You basically just do rib on those 6 sts all the way up to the top.

>

Just to explain › *RS row › BUTT, k1 tbl, p1, k1 tbl, p1, k1 tbl, p1, then k1 as a kind of edge st in middle of piece. Knit pattern repeat until 2 (4) 2 (4) 2 (4) 2 (4) remain, work these in main colour. Turn. WS row › Work 2 (4) 2 (4) 2 (4) 2 (4) sts in main colour, continue pattern until 7 sts remain. p1, p1 tbl, k1, p1 tbl, k1, p1 tbl, k1*. Rep from * to * until you have completed the same number of pattern repeats as on the back, minus three or four (depending on how deep you want the V-neck). End on last WS-row of pattern repeat. Turn. Now for the V-neck. Yay! Simply work button band over 6 sts as before, k2tog (p. 244), work pattern. When reading colour chart, don't forget to account for sts cast off through decreases. Basically, that means starting at a different place in the colour chart with every dec. Work rest of WS row and dec on front as before until you have same number of pattern repeats as on back. Last row is WS row. Work 1st 6 sts in rib for button band, cast off remaining sts in main colour. Place sts of button band on stitch holder. Work left side of front in exactly the same way but in reverse. Work in rib, as with right side of front. Switch to needle size 7, *BUTT, k1 (3) 1 (3) 1 (3) 1 (3) in main colour, work pattern according to colour chart until 7 sts remain, k1, k1 tbl, p1, k1 tbl, p1, k1 tbl, k1. Turn. BUTT, p1 tbl, k1, p1 tbl, k1, p1 tbl, k1, work pattern according to colour chart until 2 (4) 2 (4) 2 (4) 2 (4) sts remain. p1 (3) 1 (3) 1 (3) 1 (3), end with k1. Rep these 2 rows from * until decs begin for neck. Work as with right front, but with decs for V-neck at end of row, just before button band. Work edge sts and pattern as before until 8 sts remain. SKP (p. 244), work button band as before. When reading colour chart, remember to account for sts that have disappeared through decs. Basically, that means starting at a different place in the colour chart with every dec. Work WS rows as before. Continue as with right front until you have same number of pattern repeats and work is same length. Cast off in main colour with RS facing, as far as button band. Work button band, then place sts on stitch holder.

Shoulder seams (sweater and cardy) ★ Lay back and front(s) with wrong sides facing towards each other. Using main colour and crochet hook, close shoulder seams with slip stitch (p. 244). *Right shoulder ›* Start on outside of right shoulder. Close first seam. To do this, push hook through outer loop (p. 248) so the seam doesn't come out too bulky. Crochet not to loosely and not too tightly. Keep crocheting until all sts on front have been used (except sts on stitch holder, if you are making cardy). Cut off yarn. *Left shoulder ›* Again, close seams with RS facing. Count same number of sts on cast-off edges of left front and back. Start from neck and crochet until all sts of front have been used. Cut off yarn. This way, both seams will look the same. Beautiful! If you have a few excess sts on one shoulder, who will ever know? Maybe you were watching telly and miscounted. No matter. Just keep going. That's happened to me more than once, including with some of the garments shown in this book. When the music plays and, you know...

Sleeves (sweater and cardy) ★ I find it easiest and nicest to knit the sleeves straight on. To do that, pick up sts on side edges. The outside end of the shoulder seam will be the middle of your picked-up sts. Normally, I always recommend picking up fewer sts than there are rows. But this sweater is the exception that confirms the rule. The sleeve shape is nicest, of course, if you pick up 1 st per row. Start with right sleeve: Spread front(s) and back out flat on table or floor. Count 26 (28) 30 (32) 34 (36) 38 (40) rows from shoulder seam down, along edge of back. Here, start picking up sts – but not straight from BUTT! Instead, with size 7 needle, pick up sts from most visible sts you can see along edge, probably 2 or 3 sts in from edge. Using main colour, pick up 26 (28) 30 (32) 34 (36) 38 (40) sts. You should now be at the shoulder seam. Continue on other side of shoulder seam, picking up another 26 (28) 30 (32) 34 (36) 38 (40) sts in the same column of sts as on back. *You now have all your sts for right sleeve ›* = 52 (56) 60 (64) 68 (72) 76 (80) sts

>

When I knit crazy stripes, I knit both sleeves or both fronts at the same time so they come out the same. LOL

Fake it 'til you make it!

Another ombre, only this time not in subtle shades (like on p. 134) but in a mix of whatever yarns I thought were cool that day.

Next row = WS row: BUTT, p to last st, k1, turn. Now work pattern in rows, with edge sts as for front/back (= BUTT on 1st st, k1 on last st). For the perfect sweater, turn the colour chart upside down. Or not. k1 (3) 1 (3) 1 (3) 1 (3), start pattern repeat with RS facing. Pick up pattern colour, work pattern according to instructions until 2 (4) 2 (4) 2 (4) 2 (4) sts remain. k1 (3) 1 (3) 1 (3) 1 (3), end with k1 (= edge st). Turn. With WS facing › BUTT, p1 (3) 1 (3) 1 (3) 1 (3). Work pattern according to instructions, p last 2 (4) 2 (4) 2 (4) 2 (4) sts. p1 (3) 1 (3) 1 (3) 1 (3), k1 on final st (edge st). Rep these 2 rows with pattern in k and p + edge st until you have completed 5-7 pattern repeats down sleeve (or until sleeve is required length). Last row = WS row. Turn. Continue in main colour. BUTT, k1, k2tog, *k2, k2tog*, rep from * to * until all sts are worked. Turn = 39 (42) 45 (48) 51 (54) 57 (60) sts. p 1 row and work edge st. Now work ribbing as for front(s) and back. Switch to needle size 6. For sizes 1, 3, 5 and 7: On 1st row, straight after BUTT, k2tog tbl to create an even number of sts. Work 4-7 cm or desired length in rib. Cast off in rib.

Knit left sleeve in same way, counting down front (not back) from shoulder seam to pick up sts.

V-neck (sweater) ★ Start in middle of back, with RS facing out. Using circular needle size 6, pick up 1 st per st/row all the way round neck hole. Use either outer or inner loop of edge sts. Both options are fine, but choose one and stick with it. When you get to the two cast-off sts in middle of V-neck, pick up 1 new st from horizontal thread between them. This is the middle st. Mark it if you wish. I can't tell you exactly how many sts to pick up round the neck, as there are countless possible variations. But make sure it is an even number and that you have the same number on both sides of the middle st. Work in rib (k1 tbl, p1) until 1 st before middle st. Slip 2 st tog knitwise loosely, k1, pass 2 slipped sts over just-knitted st. You have now completed your first V-neck decrease. Work st straight after dec in same way as st right before dec. Sounds cryptic but basically means this: if you k1 before dec, k1 after it too. If you p1 before it, p1 after it, of course. Rep dec in every round. Work 6-8 rnds until you are pleased with the result. Cast off in rib (k above k, p above p).

Finish button band (cardy) ★ Count number of cast-off sts on back of neck, between left and right shoulder seams. If there are, say, 14 sts, you will need to work another seven rows of rib

The button bands meet and are joined.

Brill V-neck, although I say it myself.

on each side of the button band, as you need 2 rows for each edge st, for joining. Work to suit the neck so that the button band doesn't come out baggy. If you have 16 sts, you will need to work 8 rows, etc. Start with button band on left side of right front. Move 6 sts from stitch holder onto needle size 6 and continue in rib in main colour (with edge sts). Work required number of rows, cut off yarn, return sts to stitch holder. Knit button band on left front in same way. Leave sts on needle when done. Move sts of right button band onto another needle size 6, knit together with sts of other button band, casting off as you go. Join button band to back of neck by crocheting together in main colour. Push hook first through outer loop, then through inner one on back of neck. On button band, push hook only through outer loop. That way your 14 cast-off sts will now fit with your 7 "new" sts. Cut off yarn, knot and sew in ends.

Assembly (sweater and cardy) ★ Knot and sew in the ends. Lay front(s), back and sleeves on top of each other with wrong sides facing inwards and front(s) on top. With RS facing and crochet hook size 6, use main colour to close side and sleeve seams in slip stitch (p. 244). Push the hook through the outer loop of the BUTT (p. 248). Crochet not too tightly and not too loosely either. Start on bottom edge of cuff, crochet up to bottom of armhole (sleeve seam) and then down to bottom edge of sweater/ cardy (side seam). Crochet seam on other side in opposite direction, i.e. from bottom edge up to cuff. That will give you a nice, symmetrical finish as both seams will point in the same direction.

Instructions

Fancy Tube Top

Random stripes as the main colour and black as the pattern colour.

Basic yarn ★ *Basic yarn 1 (main colour)* › 1 strand Arwetta or 1 strand Mille Colori Baby alone. *Basic yarn 2 (pattern colour)* › 1 strand Arwetta alone (Yarn types and alternatives, p. 254).

Scrap yarn ★ Varying lengths of thick, thin, smooth and shaggy yarns, wound to balls or skeins (p. 234). Ideally, use yarns that suit needle size 3-3.5 so that the pattern doesn't come out wavy. Scrap yarn and Arwetta for knitting stripes, if desired.

Size ★ 1 (2) 3 (4) 5 (6) 7 (8) (Size guide, p. 239).

Chest measurement of garment ★ Approx. 61 (67) 74 (80) 86 (92) 98 (104) cm. This measurement is the total circumference measured just under the armhole when the top is laid out flat on a table.

Total length ★ Long or short, you decide. If you are knitting with the specified tension, one pattern repeat will be about 3 cm long. Plus the ribbing. For a short top, I find a same-sized (e.g. 2-3 cm) band of ribbing top and bottom looks best. For a longer top, I think a wider (4-6 cm) band of ribbing at the bottom and a narrower one (2-3 cm) at the top looks better.

Yarn requirement ★ *Basic yarn 1 (main colour)* › At least 1 ball Arwetta or Mille Colori Baby. *Basic yarn 2 (pattern colour)* › At least 1 ball Arwetta. *Scrap yarn* › At least 50 g.

Needles ★ Circular needle size 3.5, 60-80 cm (for pattern), circular needle size 3, 60-80 cm (for ribbing), dpn size 3 (for straps).

Tension square ★ Approx. 26 sts and 28-30 rows of pattern on needle size 3.5 = 10 x 10 cm. (Tension, p. 239). If your gauge is different, use thicker or thinner needles.

Colour chart D p. 129

A fancy little tube top knitted on thin needles. Measure your chest and knit one size smaller. The top needs to be a snug fit. It is knitted entirely in rounds, so it's ideal for making while you are on the go. Add straps (p. 44) or not, as you wish. Knit the top as part of a set, for instance with a matching bag (p. 126) or jacket (p. 132). Reinforce the top edge, with some elastic, perhaps, so your top doesn't end up slipping down (p. 46). I knitted the main colour in stripes with various scrap yarns and some Awetta, but you can also knit the pattern colour in stripes, which will give you a "calmer" look.

>

With straps (p. 44).

Basic instructions

Front and back ★ Cast on 160 (176) 192 (208) 224 (240) 256 (272) sts on circular needle size 3. Place marker at beg of rnd. Close to form rnd and continue in rib (k1 tbl, p1). *Round 1* › Work 80 (88) 96 (104) 112 (120) 128 (136) sts, place marker (= other side of top). Work in rib to desired length. Switch to circular needle size 3.5, work pattern in main and pattern colours as shown in colour chart. Continue until work is desired length, minus top ribbing. Switch to circular needle size 3 and work top ribbing in same way as bottom ribbing. When you have knitted the desired length, cast off in rib (k above k, p above p). If you intend to add straps, leave markers in place.

Straps ★ Lay top out flat with side markers in place. *Front right strap* › Count 10 (10 (12) 12 (14) 14 (16) 16 sts from marker to middle. Starting with this st, use dpn size 3 to pick up 2 (2) 2 (3) 3 (4) 4 (4) sts from edge (through both loops of st). Work in k, as for I-cord, i.e. rather than turning at end of row, push sts to other end of needle and change hands. Bring yarn across back of work to the front, k all sts. Knitting in one direction like this pulls the sts together to form a tube. Work to desired length. Leave an end of approx. 10 cm, cut off yarn and thread end into a darning needle. Push needle clockwise through sts to cast off. Carefully pull tight, knot end and cut off yarn. Work left strap in same way. If desired, add straps to back as well, which you can tie with front ones on tops of shoulders (Straps, p. 44).

Barbie Knit

That haircut, those ear-rings, that coat and that Leo overall - I want them NOW!

Fancy Cardy/Sweater

Basic yarn ★ *Basic yarn 1 (main colour)* › 1 strand Arwetta or Mille Colori Baby alone. *Basic yarn 2 (pattern colour)* › 1 strand Arwetta plus 1 strand scrap yarn (Yarn types and alternatives, p. 254).

Scrap yarn ★ Varying lengths of thin silk mohair and sewing cotton, wound into a small skein. I wind skeins of scrap yarn all the time. You don't need much for this.

Size ★ One size.

Yarn requirement ★ At least 20 g each of main and pattern colours.

Needles ★ Size 3 (It's up to you whether you use circular or straight needles to knit in rows), crochet hook size 3 for assembly.

Technique ★ Houndstooth pattern, see p. 121 for details.

Basic instructions

Back (cardy and sweater) ★ Cast on 26 sts in main colour on needle size 3. Continue in rib (k1 tbl, p1) in rows. Use pattern colour to knit pattern. BUTT (always and forever), rep houndstooth pattern 3 times across work, k1. 1st and last sts are edge sts. (Knit main and pattern colours together on edges, p. 80.) Continue in pattern until work is desired length. I knitted 6½ patterns up the garment, but you can also knit less. Cast off knitwise in main colour.

Front(s) (cardy and sweater) ★ For sweater: knit front in exactly the same way as back. Doing a V-neck on a Barbie knit is tricky. But she'll deal with it.

Right front (cardy) Cast on 12 sts on needle size 3, and work in rib, as for back. BUTT, 3 sts in rib (front edge), one pattern repeat across piece, finishing with k1. Continue until you have the same number of pattern repeats as on back. Cast off with RS facing. Work left front in exactly the same way, but in reverse, with the front edge on the other side of the piece.

Close shoulder seams as shown on p. 248. If knitting sweater, make sure hole in middle is big enough for Barbie/Ken's head.

Sleeves ★ Knit sleeves onto front and back as described on p. 138: pick up 34 sts (= 17 sts on each side of shoulder seam). BUTT, p 1 row. Next row: BUTT, work pattern repeat 4 times across piece, k1. Continue until work is 2 pattern repeats long. Next row: k2tog until end of row = 17 sts, half the number you had before. Work 5 rows in rib, cast off. Knit second sleeve in exactly the same way.

Rollneck ★ For sweater, knit fold-down rollneck if you like: with dpn size 3, pick up 1 st per row all the way round neck hole, work 12 rounds in rib. Cast off, fold neck down.

Assembly ★ Close side and sleeve seams as described on p. 248. Knot the ends. Mwah!

Knitting a V-neck for Barbie is tricky. I'm sure she will manage with what she has.

Chapter 4

He dies. Imagine. I carried my father's coffin. A note on how needles and yarns told the stories I couldn't tell myself.

At midday on 31 July 2016 my phone rang. It was an unknown number calling from abroad. I was on parental leave with my seven-month-old daughter Lulu at the time and happened to be in Aalborg, visiting my parents. At the time I hadn't seen or spoken to my father for three years. He didn't even know I had become a mother. On the phone, he told me he was ill and going to die. He had another year at most. He also said that he had been aware of the fact for the last six months but not known how to tell me. That was the first time I ever heard him cry.

The last time we had seen each other – three years earlier – we parted on bad terms after a huge argument at Nørreport station. He was just about to go back to Greenland after two terrible days of nastiness, misunderstandings and accusations. We had been calling each other all sorts of horrible and hurtful things, and it felt as though the tenuous tie between us had worn thin and broken completely. It just didn't hold anymore. So, he got on the bus to the airport, and I went off to visit a friend, where I then spent two days in tears on her couch. I was broken, devastated and furious. I also knew 100 percent that I couldn't stand it any longer and needed to get away from him for a while. I needed time to care for myself and would have to retreat, even though I didn't really want to.

He was noticeably different too. Much angrier with the world than usual. But of course, he didn't tell me why. All I could do was guess. Most of all, I wanted to be even more committed to earning him as my father, to fight harder, invest more, be softer. But I also knew I would be fighting on my own. He had given up. I reckon he thought, "Well, I'm moving back home in a couple of years anyway, so we can sort it out then. Make a fresh start. I can't do that anymore at the moment."

Time passed. I met Sune, the love of my life, graduated from Design School and became a mother. And my dad knew nothing of any of it. Until he called me on 31 July 2016. I was shocked. I had no idea what to do. I thought we had more time. That's what you always think. Until you don't anymore. He thought we had more time too. I took a photo of Lulu and me and sent it straight to him. I also asked him to send a photo of himself to me. He said he would be coming to Denmark for treatment in a few weeks' time, and we arranged to meet up.

Incidentally, the week he called to tell me he was going to die was also the week I set up my own business. So, I had no secure income and had to be sensible, focused, driven, creative and believe in myself. And all at a time in my life when I was absolutely none of those things.

I took a bus to Søborg to meet him. I'll never forget sitting there, on the bus in Søborg Hovedgade, looking out of the window. Without actually seeing anything. It was as though none of it was really happening. I felt like I was in an absurd film – which I was watching at the same time. It's not a very good film, I thought to myself as I sat there, on the bus. So full of cliches and banal.

I had no idea what to expect. What would my dad look like? How sick and how different would he be? I hadn't seen him for the past three years, and I was a completely different person too: I now had a family, had graduated and had a baby. And yet I was still his little girl, his child, forever.

He looked ill. He had shrunk and grown thinner, and he seemed fragile – despite doing his best to hide behind his big, bushy beard. But most of all he seemed weak. He was there, but not really. He looked me in the eye – briefly – but then looked back down again every time. He suddenly seemed ashamed of his illness. Maybe he felt guilty towards me? He asked me to tell him about Lulu and Sune, but I could also sense that he didn't want to hear, see or know too much. Maybe it was too painful for him. It probably would have been for me.

We arranged for him to come for dinner at our house so he could meet my family. And he also wanted to plan his funeral with me, by the way, and asked when I would have time. I mean, what do you say to a question like that? "Thursday at 5 would be great for planning your funeral." I told him to choose a time.

The first time he met Lulu and Sune, my mind went completely blank. All I remember is thinking he was clearly better at dealing with little kids than with grown-up ones. Or maybe with kids that weren't me. He played with Lulu a lot, and Sune said he clearly enjoyed his time with us. I constantly wanted to know what Sune was thinking, seeing and experiencing. I simply couldn't feel, see or experience anything for myself.

I actually had quite a lot of mental blanks that autumn. Great big black holes into which time and experiences just disappeared. Days and weeks I simply don't remember at all. I was on autopilot the whole time, and my sense of time was dominated by my contact with my father. When I saw him, when he called, when he wrote. And how he wanted me to help.

He to-ed and fro-ed between Greenland and Denmark for his treatment in the Rigshospitalet. I could feel he needed me. He felt lonely

The first time my dad met Lulu.

and scared but was unable to find a way of letting me in. I didn't get the sense he was opening up and letting me take on the role I had so wished for in his life. Instead, he complained that I had bought him the wrong prepaid card and washed his T-shirts wrong. He was angry. I really understood that. And he didn't want to talk to me about his condition, treatment or when he would be returning to Greenland. Being his daughter was difficult.

During this period, my handicrafts were my only refuge. They were the only thing that had no expectations of me. Knitting neither took energy, nor did it demand responsibility from me. My grief was – and still is – lonely. Other people said they understood me and got where I was coming from. But they can't have because they had no real understanding of the grief I was going through. Although I know they would have liked to. But my handicrafts understood me. My knitting understood, and my needles listened, with their familiar clicking, and did what I told them to do, no questions asked, no answers expected.

On 3 November 2016 my phone rang again. And again it was an unknown number. I was at work – knitting – in my new workshop in Nørrebro. The call was him. I could immediately hear he was in a foul mood. He told me he was going back to Greenland the next day and that he couldn't stand it in goddam Copenhagen any longer! He said the place was making him even sicker, and he didn't want any more treatment. He just wanted to go home, he said, and if I wanted to say goodbye, I would have to do it now because otherwise he would not have time. So, if *I* wanted to say goodbye, I would have to come NOW. There was no mention of *him* wanting to say goodbye.

Without giving it a second thought, I immediately called a taxi and went over to the patients' hotel in Østerbro. There we spent half an hour sitting in the common room together, while the handball was on the television. He was in a dreadful mood. He told me what he had been given for lunch, a Danish steamed cabbage dish called Stuvet Hvidkål, and we talked about the way his grandma used to make it. I didn't say much. There wasn't much to say, really. I just remember thinking, look at him. Look at him now! Because soon you won't be able to anymore.

At some point he stood up and announced he was tired and needed to pack. The visit was over, and it was time for me to go, he said. He saw me out. As we stood outside, he said, "See you." I found the idea of leaving unbearable, so I just stood there and started to cry. I knew it would be the last time I saw him. And he knew it too. We would never see each other again. "Off you go," he said and smiled at me for the first time in weeks. There were tears in his eyes, and I could just about see them, even though he didn't want me to. He turned round, and I walked away. I couldn't feel my body anymore. All I could do was cry as I walked. After 20 metres I turned round to wave to him, but he had already gone inside.

Sune took this photo of me when I was writing the chapter you are reading right now.

I never saw him again. He went back to Greenland and switched off his phone for three weeks. I couldn't reach him. A first I thought he was dead, but then I realised someone would have told me by now. I texted him and tried to call him every evening, but his phone was "out of service". Until finally, one evening, it was no longer "out of service" and he answered. "Hey, what do you want?" he asked. I replied that I had not heard from him for over three weeks. He flew into a rage and said all he wanted was his peace and quiet. We chatted for a few minutes – about the weather in Greenland. Then he said he was tired, so we hung up.

On 18 December 2016 my phone rang. It was an unknown number calling from abroad. I was just on my way to Aalborg to celebrate Christmas with my parents and Lulu. Sune would be joining us in a few days' time. The last time I had spoken to my father was a week before, on Lulu's first birthday. He had called to wish her a happy birthday, but at a very inopportune moment. I was a bit short with him and said I would call him back. But I didn't. I forgot. Well, actually, no that's not true. I simply didn't have the strength to do it. I was tired, exhausted by the grief, disappointment and responsibility. I was drained and very tired. This time, though, it wasn't my dad on the phone but his girlfriend from Greenland. I immediately knew what had happened. She told me my dad had died the day before. He had simply fallen in his house in Sydprøven, while he was on his own, and later been found by a friend. He hadn't suffered, she said. So, there I was with my little one-year-old and no idea what to do next.

His coffin was brought over from Greenland, and the funeral was planned for 4 January 2017. There was a time when he had wanted to be buried up in Greenland. But I found the thought unbearable. Luckily, he changed his mind and wanted to be buried in northern Jutland instead. Maybe because he could sense how much he mattered to so many of us.

Sune and I drove to the church, which was right next to the house my father had bought but never lived in. The house I never visited – and that I first saw at the wake after his funeral. My dad had planned to move in when he got back from Greenland. He had also planned for us to grow closer. A new beginning, as he would call it. But we never made it.

Carrying my father's coffin, I was completely out of it. Totally gone. During his lifetime he had laid claim to everything. And now, in death, it felt as though he was taking every last crumb of me with him. It was as though all that was left was a false little girl.

I can hardly remember the funeral – except for the fact that we couldn't sing *Septembers himmel er så blå* (The September Sky Is So Blue) because it wasn't in the hymn book. It was the only goddam song he wanted sung at his funeral – he told me when we were planning it together – and he didn't get it! I am still ashamed of that, even now. It feels like I had let him down again and would only ever be a terrible daughter.

I remember thinking, "What the hell, Lærke! Just smile. This is so sad it's unbearable."

I remember how heavy his coffin was. I had insisted on being one of the pall bearers – because that was what I wanted. Even if everyone did tell me the coffin would be too heavy and there was really no need. And it really was heavy, so heavy I could hardly lift it – despite the fact that there were five grown men carrying it with me. But I wanted to help carry it. It was the least I could do for him. And it was my last chance to be close to him, even if he was lying in his coffin. The film in my head started playing again, and I thought, what a terrible actress I was! Just crying all the time!

Afterwards we walked the short way to his house. Inside the house, everything was him: the Hamsun books, the blue coffeepots, the Neil Young CDs. There were some things I could still remember, others he had bought later, but they looked as though they had always been there. I didn't want to be there. But nor did I want to leave. I hadn't seen most of the guests for more than 15 years. I was expected to chat with them – which I did, as if my life depended on me being in a house where I had never visited him before, right after his funeral. I had never felt so lonely in all my life.

When everything was over, Sune and I drove home to Aalborg. I fell silent. I was thinking about him lying under the ground and how cold he must be. I forgot he was dead and couldn't actually feel the cold anymore. When I got home, I picked up Lulu and went back to being a mother, not a daughter. I took my knitting and decided to make something challenging. Not super-challenging, just slightly challenging. I needed it. So, I knitted a technique called entrelac. My body started to relax, my breathing grew calm, my belly grew softer. I didn't really know where I was going with my knitting, I had no plan. I just knitted square after square. And enjoyed it. I knitted out what I could not put into words. I was knitting my grief out of my body.

I didn't really know where I was going with my knitting, I had no plan. I just knitted square after square. And enjoyed it. I knitted out what I could not put into words. I was knitting my grief out of my body. My handicrafts understood me. My knitting understood, and my needles listened, with their familiar clicking, and did what I told them to do, no questions asked, no answers expected.

Drawings and sketches of entrelac.

Entrelac

From here on in, things are going to get a little tricky. But that's fine. After all, no one said it would be plain sailing all the way. And challenging things are often a way of stepping back for a while. Maybe you need a break? I need quite a lot of them, actually. So, when life throws difficult stuff at me, I like to get stuck into my knitting, which can also be a little be difficult. No, knitting is never more difficult than life itself. Of course not. But it does provide a little distraction. Maybe it's a bit of an escape? Or just a chance for a bit of a breather? Quite honestly, there's nothing wrong with using your handicrafts as a bit of an escape. Knitting is good for the soul. And it's more than just dipping in: knitting is your very own world. Sometimes knitting is extroverted. And sometimes it's introverted. Just like us people. Just like you and me.

In the months when my father was ill (and I knew about it), up to his death, I so needed to escape and to immerse myself into my own world. It was a way of escaping the responsibility and finding the space to take a few nice deep breaths and get away from all the crying and worries. And so I decided to try entrelac knitting. I have a twenty-year-old book that describes the technique. It may even have been my first knitting book.

Entrelac has me spellbound. It's just so damn beautiful! But I was equally attracted by the fact that it was so challenging: mastering entrelac, trying it via the Lærke Bagger machine and seeing what comes out. I really wanted to know how it's done. But it was challenging. The description was so difficult and complicated, but I had had my eye on it for years.

Knit square after square. No strings attached. You can always change your mind tomorrow. Or use a different colour or technique. Just do what feels right.

When my father's condition became incurable, when there was no hope at all of him recovering and it was just a question of time until he died, entrelac was just what I needed. It came at exactly a time in my life when I had to shoulder the greatest responsibility and felt I had to grow up and face up to the difficult tasks that lay ahead.

Maybe you are not at a point like this in your life at the moment. Maybe things are going just fine with you, and you don't want to be dragged down by difficult topics. In that case, just look at the lovely pictures. Because who knows? Entrelac might be exactly what you need. Maybe this is the perfect time and you feel ready for a cool challenge like this. And hey, it's not *that* difficult anyway. So, why not just give it a try and see what comes out?

The fact that there are more than nine more pages of technique to go is pretty hard to bear, I know. Bummer. But entrelac is fun and one of my absolute favourite techniques. So carry on reading! Entrelac is worth all nine pages!

Entrelac looks like a patchwork or a basket-woven effect. I say basket-woven because that's what I think it looks like. It's done by knitting row upon row of half and full squares in alternating directions. Every square is created by picking up stitches from the square below it. The stitches are then knitted in rows and knitted together with the stitches of the square beneath. Sounds confusing, right? Don't worry, it's great fun to do (and easy as well), once you've got the hang of it. Let me show you. We're in this together!

This technique has a certain je-ne-sais-quoi about it. Square after square, colour after colour, call after call, text after text, hour after hour, day after day.

When my dad was on his deathbed, entrelac quite simply made sense to me. It helped me through my grief, desperation and regrets. It opened my eyes to the fact that there was no quick fix for the relationship between my dad and me and that I would need to give myself time. The grief stayed with me. For a long time. Maybe forever. Square after square as I continued to grieve.

One day I would knit squares in dark, gloomy colours, the next I would use bright, fresh, optimistic shades. It was a way of knitting out my sorrow and fears, my sadness and desperation. But also the little signs of progress that I was experiencing. My knitting grew out of my body and became a mirror of my moods and thoughts. I told stories through it that I would otherwise never have been able to tell. For which I had no words. Which I can only tell now, five years after he died.

Because all the squares are knitted individually, entrelac is a great opportunity to play around with textures, colours, techniques and materials. In other words, make it your own, baby! Every time you have knitted (half) a square and want to change yarn, just cut off the end and start with a new strand. It's a brilliant way of giving your scraps an awesome second life. Yes, I can hear you saying, "Oh, but there will be so many ends to sew in!" But luckily all we are doing is tying knots… you can do entrelac not just in stocking stitch but in other techniques as well. See every square as a new chance to shine and show what you can do, as a blank sheet of paper that's better than the one that went before. Try out new ideas. More on that later, though. For now, let's just start with the basics.

Entrelac opened my eyes to the fact that there was no quick fix for the relationship between my dad and me and that I would need to give myself time. The grief stayed with me. For a long time. Maybe forever. Square after square as I continued to grieve.

How to knit entrelac

Entrelac consists of four different tiers of squares that are all knitted in different ways but based on the same principle:

Tier 1 (start): Half-squares
Tier 2: Right-leaning half and full squares
Tier 3: Left-leaning full squares
Final tier: Half-squares

The first row is only knitted at the start, and the final row is only knitted at the end. Between the two you knit nothing but rows of right- and left-leaning squares – over and over again.

As with almost all my knitting patterns, good edge stitches are essential if you want your work to look neat and tidy. And of course, my recommendation is to finish each row with a BUTT. But you can also just do the edges in whatever way you like best.

The squares and half-squares are all knitted with the same number of stitches. The more stitches in a square, the longer and wider it will be. In other words, if you want to knit an entrelac piece comprising three squares, each one 10 stitches across, you will need to cast on 3 x 10 stitches. That's 30 stitches in total. You can knit an odd or even number of squares and make them bigger or smaller than the 10 stitches I just mentioned as an example.

I think it's a great idea to try this technique out before embarking on a huge coat or pullover. You could try and make something like a cute little pillow (p. 174).

You can knit entrelac in rows or rounds. Here, I have decided to only demonstrate it in rows. Partly because that's the way I have always done it, and partly because that's the way I like it best. It also works for most designs.

So, entrelac. Give it a whirl. It's SOOO great to do! I suggest trying it out on 6-7 mm needles (because then, if you like it, you can turn your knitting into a cushion cover, p. 174). The stitches will be big enough for you to easily see what you are doing. You can learn a lot by observing your own technique as you knit and seeing what comes out at the end. You can always modify and adapt things later, whenever you like.

Here comes a suggestion for knitting entrelac with three squares that are each 10 stitches wide.

Follow the instructions step by step for the individual tiers, checking the images to help you. Imagine the open stitches are on a needle. You might also want to try and use different materials and colours for each square as you go.

Cast on 30 stitches using the right needle size for your yarn. So far, so good. You can use a circular needle too, but bear in mind that you will be knitting in rows, not rounds.

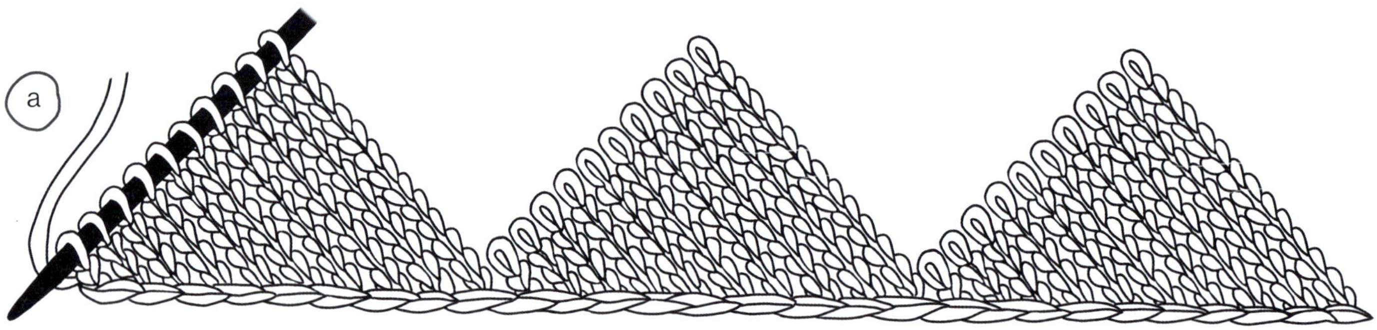

Tier 1 (start): Half-squares (a)

Create the first half-square with RS facing.

Rows 1 and 2 › k2, turn, BUTT, k1, turn
Rows 3 and 4 › BUTT, k2, turn, BUTT, p1, k1, turn.
Rows 5 and 6 › BUTT, k3, turn, BUTT, p2, k1, turn.
Rows 7 and 8 › BUTT, k4, turn, BUTT, p3, k1, turn.
Rows 9 and 10 › BUTT, k5, turn, BUTT, p4, k1, turn.
Rows 11 and 12 › BUTT, k6, turn, BUTT, p5, k1, turn.
Rows 13 and 14 › BUTT, k7, turn, BUTT, p6, k1, turn.
Rows 15 and 16 › BUTT, k8, turn, BUTT, p7, k1, turn.
Row 17 › BUTT, k9, don't turn.

You now have 10 stitches on your right needle (and 20 on your left one), and your first half-square is complete.

In principle, on every RS row, you are knitting one stitch more off your left needle and onto your right one. This means you will gradually have more and more stitches on your right needle until you finally have the number you have chosen for each square (in this case, 10 stitches).

With your first half-square now done, leave the stitches on your right needle and move on. If you are changing colour or yarn for the next square, you might want to cut the yarn. Knit the next two half-squares in exactly the same way as the first one. If you do everything right, you will end up having worked all 30 of your cast-on stitches and with three half-squares on your right needle. Turn your work.

Great, now we're up and running.

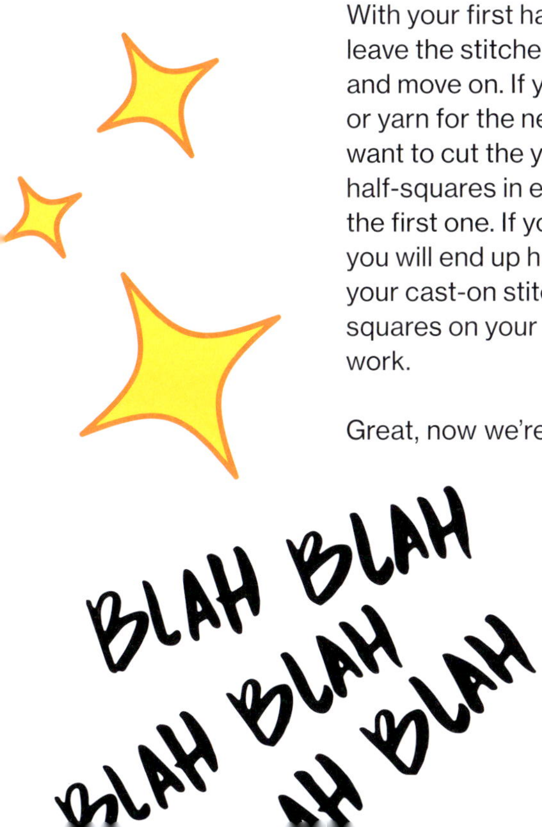

Tier 2: Right-leaning half- and full squares

So that your knitting has straight edges, this tier will always have a half-square at the beginning and end. Work with WS facing.

Half-square on left edge (b)
Rows 1 and 2 › p1, k1, turn, BUTT, k1, turn.
Rows 3 and 4 › pfb (= inc 1, see p. 244), k2tog (using 1 st from "new" square and 1 st from half-square below it), turn, BUTT, k2, turn.
Rows 5 and 6 › BUTT, pfb, k2tog, turn, BUTT, k3, turn.
Rows 7 and 8 › BUTT, pfb, p1, k2tog, turn, BUTT, k4 turn.
Rows 9 and 10 › BUTT, pfb, p2, k2tog, turn BUTT, k5, turn.
Rows 11 and 12 › BUTT, pfb, p3, k2tog, turn, BUTT k6, turn.
Rows 13 and 14 › BUTT, pfb, p4, k2tog, turn, BUTT, k7, turn.
Rows 15 and 16 › BUTT, pfb, p5, k2tog, turn, BUTT, k8, turn.
Rows 17 › BUTT, pfb, p6, k2tog, don't turn.

Basically, you are increasing one stitch at the beginning of every other row. You now have 10 stitches on your right needle (and 20 on your left one), and you have knitted each "new" stitch together with the stitch from the square below. The half-square at the edge of your second tier is finished. Now, leave the stitches on your right needle and move on. If you are changing colour or yarn, you might want to cut the yarn.

>

An ancient entrelac sweater in gorgeous colours!

Right-leaning full squares (c)
Start with WS facing. Now, with your right needle, pick up 10 stitches purl-wise evenly along the edge (i.e. from the BUTT stitches, if you did them) of the diagonal half-square below. Pick up one stitch per BUTT. For the first row, you may need to add a stitch on the edge to get the 10 stitches you need. But that will look fine.

I think it looks best if you always pick up your new stitches through the loop of the BUTT. Use the loop that's closest to you (= inner loop). That way the colour transitions won't be so bulky. Turn.

Rows 1 and 2 › k10, turn, BUTT, p8, k2tog (i.e. knit 1 stitch of the "new" square together with 1 stitch of the half-square below it), turn.
Rows 3 and 4 › BUTT, k9, turn, BUTT, p8, k2tog, turn. Repeat Rows 3 and 4 until you have knitted all the stitches of the new square together with the stitches of the square below. Your last row will be a WS row. Then, don't turn.

You now have 20 stitches on your right needle (and 10 on the left one). Now, leave the stitches on your right needle.

If you are changing colour, you might want to cut the yarn.

Knit the next square in exactly the same way. As I mentioned, you will need to create half-squares at the end of each tier so that the edges of your knitting are straight.

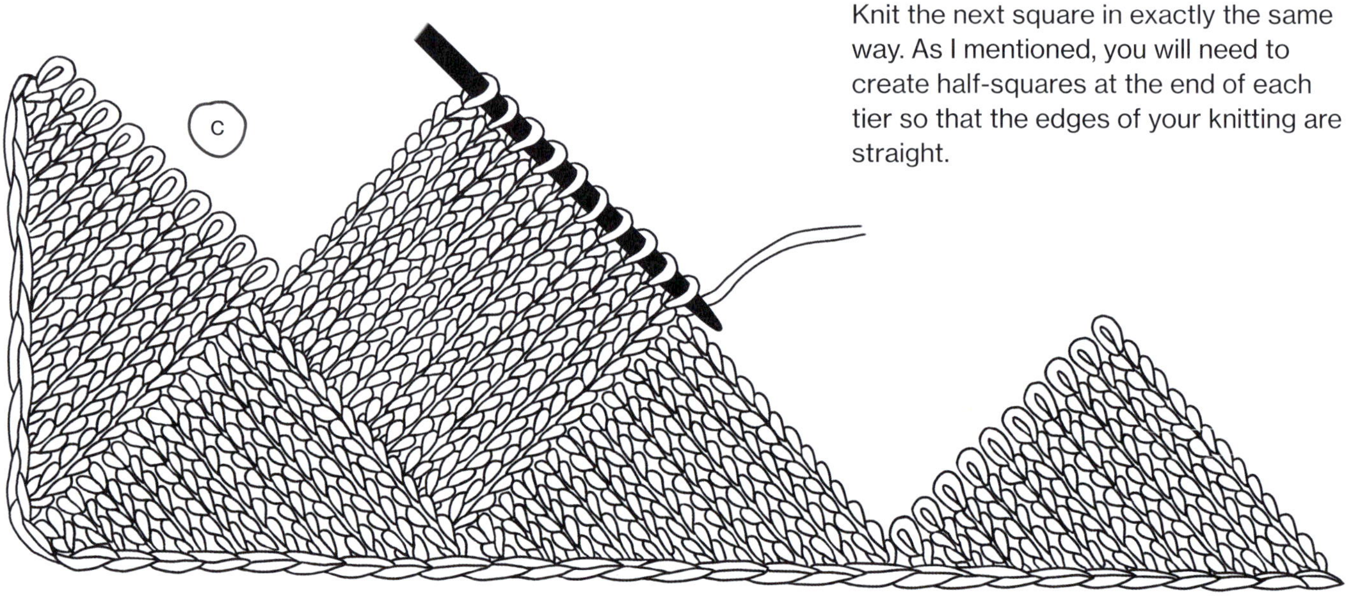

Another old knit. Here the squares are much bigger than in the instruction in this book.

Half-square on right edge (d)
Pick up 9 stitches purlwise (as described above for right-leaning full square) plus a final stitch knitwise for a neat edge. You now have 10 stitches in total.

Rows 1 and 2 › BUTT, k9, turn, BUTT, p7, k2tog (for more on decreases, see p. 244), turn.
Rows 3 and 4 › BUTT, k8, turn, BUTT p6, k2tog, turn.
Rows 5 and 6 › BUTT, k7, turn, BUTT p5, k2tog, turn.
Rows 7 and 8 › BUTT, k6, turn, BUTT, p4, k2tog, turn.
Rows 9 and 10 › BUTT, k5, turn, BUTT, p3, k2tog, turn.
Rows 11 and 12 › BUTT, k4, turn, BUTT, p2, k2tog, turn.
Rows 13 and 14 › BUTT, k3, turn, BUTT, p1, k2tog, turn.
Rows 15 and 16 › BUTT, k2, turn, BUTT, k2tog, turn.
Rows 17 and 18 › BUTT, k1, turn, k2tog.

Basically, you are now decreasing one stitch at the end of every other row. You have now knitted all the squares in your second tier. There are 31 stitches on your right needle (i.e. 10 from the half-square on the left edge, 20 from the two right-leaning squares, and 1 stitch from the half-square on the right edge). Turn.

>

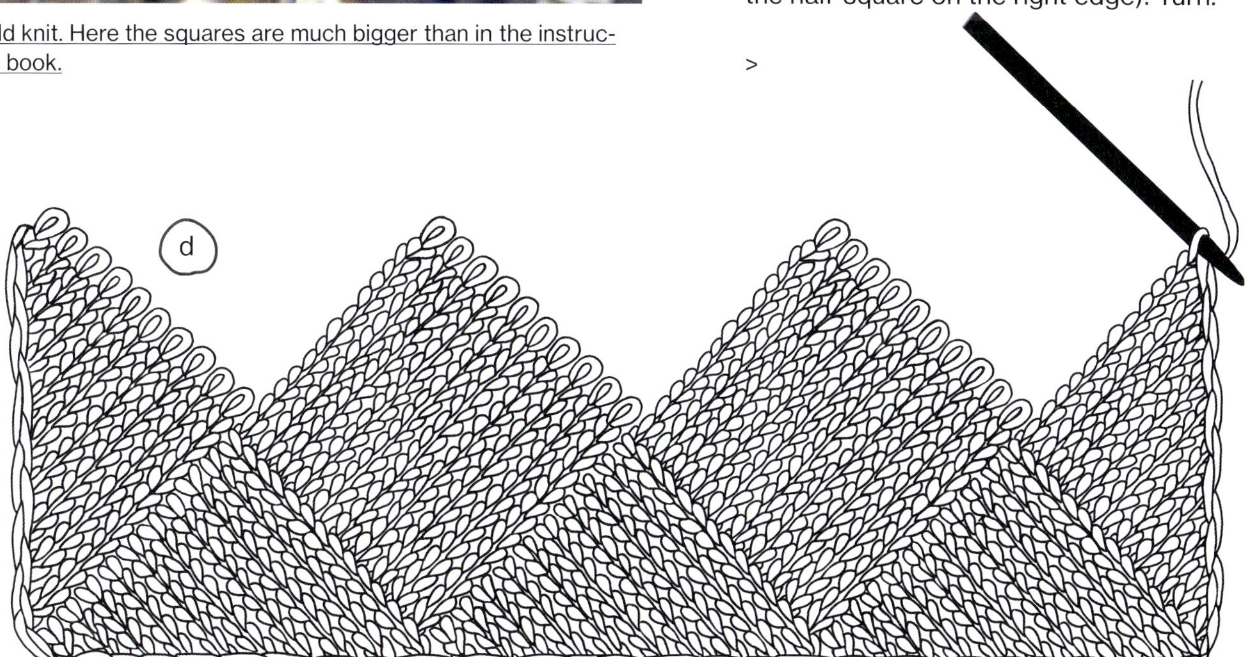

Tier 3: Left-leaning full squares

This tier consists purely of full squares. With RS facing, move the single remaining stitch on your left needle onto your right one. This is now the first stitch of your first square in this tier. So, for this particular square, you will only need to pick up another 9 stitches (9 + 1 = 10). For all other squares in this tier, you will need to pick up 10.

Left-leaning full square (e)

With RS facing, use your right needle to pick up 9 stitches knitwise (only for the first square, for all other squares pick up 10). Make sure the stitches are evenly distributed along the edge (i.e. from the BUTT stitches, if you did them) of the diagonal half-or full square below. Pick up one stitch per BUTT.

I think it looks best if you always pick up your new stitches through the loop of the BUTT. Use the loop towards the back of your knit, as this will give you a tighter edge between squares. Turn.

Rows 1 and 2 › BUTT, p8, k1, turn, BUTT, k8, k2tog (i.e. knit 1 stitch of the "new" square together with 1 stitch of the square below it), turn.

Repeat Rows 1 and 2 until all the stitches of the new square have been knitted together with the stitches of the square or half-square below. Last row = RS row. Don't turn.

You now have 10 stitches on your right needle and 20 on your left one. Now, leave the stitches on the right needle and move on. If you are changing yarn or colour, you might want to cut the yarn.

Knit the next two squares in exactly the same way (picking up 10 stitches for each one, not 9!).

You now have three beautiful left-leaning squares on your right needle. Carry on knitting.

All you have to do next is follow the instructions above to create a tier of right-leaning squares (p. 166). When that is done, you can either add further tiers of left- and right-leaning squares (e.g. to make the *Bit by Bit Pillow* on p. 174) – OR you can finish your work with a final tier of left-leaning half-squares.

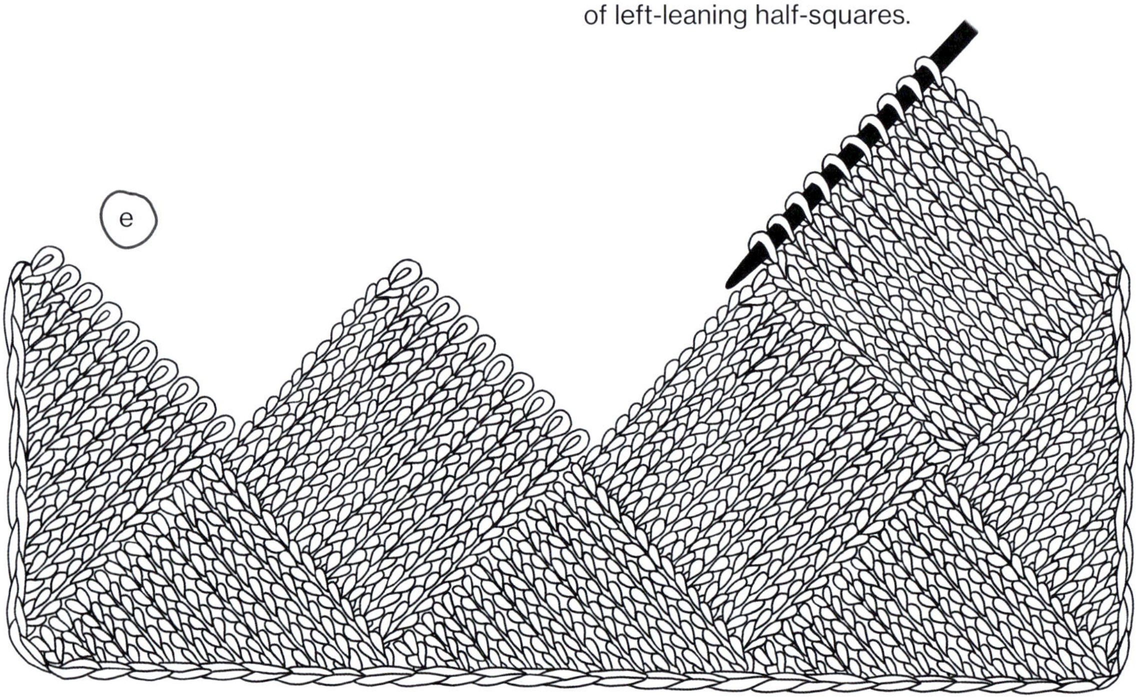

Final tier: Half-squares (f)
On this tier, you will be knitting left-leaning half-squares while casting off. With RS facing, move the single remaining stitch on your left needle onto your right one. This is the first stitch of your first half-square in this tier. After every half-square, you will be left with one stitch. This means that you only need to pick up another 9 stitches (9 + 1 = 10) for the next half-square in the final tier.

With RS facing, use your right needle to pick up 9 stitches knitwise. Make sure they are evenly distributed along the edge (i.e. from the BUTT stitches, if you did them) of the diagonal square below. Pick up one stitch per BUTT, so you have 10 sts. Turn.

Rows 1 and 2 › BUTT, p8, k1, turn, BUTT, k8, k2tog (1 stitch from the "new" square with 1 stitch from the square below), turn.
Rows 3 and 4 › BUTT, p7, k2tog, turn, BUTT, k7 k2tog, turn.
Rows 5 and 6 › BUTT, p6, k2tog, turn, BUTT, k6, k2tog, turn.
Rows 7 and 8 › BUTT, p5, k2tog, turn, BUTT, k5, k2tog, turn.
Rows 9 and 10 › BUTT, p4, k2tog, turn, BUTT, k4, k2tog, turn.
Rows 11 and 12 › BUTT, p3, k2tog, turn, BUTT, k3, k2tog, turn.
Rows 13 and 14 › BUTT, p2, k2tog, turn, BUTT, k2, k2tog, turn.
Rows 15 and 16 › BUTT, p1, k2tog, turn, BUTT, k1, k2tog, turn.
Rows 17 and 18 › BUTT, k2tog, turn, BUTT, k2tog, turn.
Rows 19 and 20 › BUTT, k2tog, don't turn.

You have now knitted the first half-square of your final tier and "cast off" at the same time. You have 1 stitch on your right needle and 20 on your left one. So, essentially, at the end of each row, you are decreasing one stitch to create half a square with a "cast-off" edge.

>

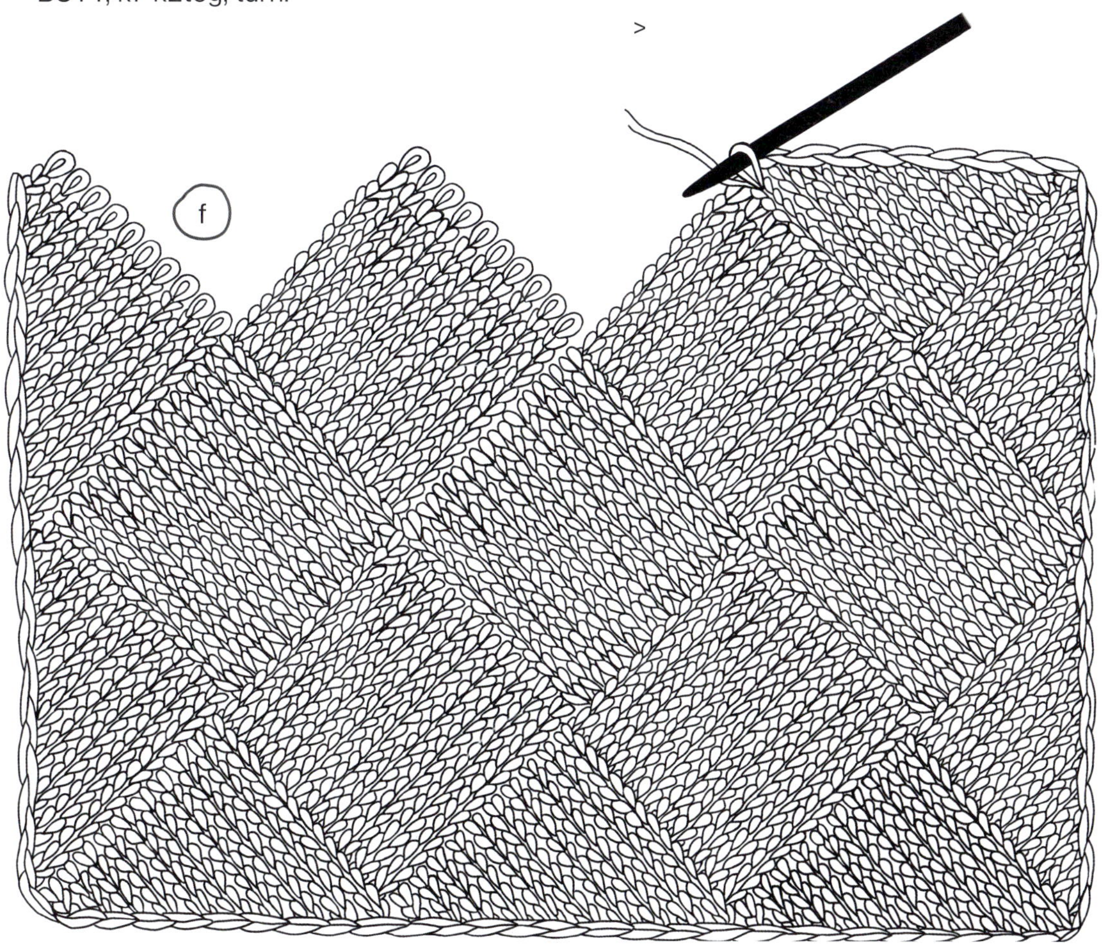

Knit the next two half-squares in exactly the same way. If you have done everything right, you will have knitted and cast off all 30 stitches and have three beautiful half-squares. You now have just one stitch left on your needle. Pull the end of the yarn through it and give yourself a huge pat on the back. It might not be the most beautiful thing you have ever knitted, but it certainly cost a lot of blood, sweat and tears, dare I say it.

Writing these instructions certainly cost me a lot of blood, sweat and tears. OMG. You think you're never going to make it! But then you do. It's a bit like grieving. In a way, at least. Maybe you or the world are not quite the same anymore, but you'll make it.

Larke, you've grown up!

When I showed my friend this sweater in these colours, she said, "Lærke, you've grown up!" The front and sleeves of a *Bit by Bit Sweater*, p. 178.

Tips on knitting entrelac

If this is your first time knitting entrelac, I certainly recommend using a light colour. That way you will be able to see the stitches better and work out where you need to pick up new ones.

You can knit entrelac squares in any size. The total number of stitches you cast on will be the number in each square multiplied by the number of squares you intend to knit. The more stitches in a square, the wider your knitting will be.

In my view there is absolutely no need to worry about mixing different types of yarn and colours. Don't think too much about your tension either. Instead, consider entrelac as an experiment in how different materials and colours work together. This technique has an old-school, patchwork style about it and needs to look handmade, if you ask me. That's because it IS handmade.

When measuring your tension square in entrelac, it's important to measure diagonally across the individual squares, not horizontally across multiple squares. Otherwise your tension square won't match the instructions. If you can't measure 10 cm, measure 5 cm instead and double it. If the edges of your entrelac work are slightly wonky, don't worry. That's life. And the seam will compensate for it. So will the ribbing, if you have any. So, take it easy.

In terms of colours, you can be flexible. You can mix an expressive 80s look in cute pastel shades with random contrasting colours. Or, if you want to be on the safe side, you can use different shades of the same colour. Or go down whatever route you like. Just find your way yourself.

Also, don't forget all the really fun yarns: the special-effect ones. Variegated yarns, fluffy yarn, yarns with glitter, shine and so on. They really enhance the look and add depth to the whole thing (Yarn types, p. 234).

Entrelac seems almost made for knitting different squares in different stitches, from stocking stitch to holes, cables, embroidered stitches, ombre, beads, sequins, whatever (p. 205). The only limiting factor is your expertise and imagination.

Stupid cut-off ends. Sigh. Just knot them. Job done. And you know what? If you take care of (i.e. knot) them as you go, it will be less bothersome at the end. I tie the cut-off bits together to make a cute little mini ball of wool which I can then knit into a square or use to make a felted bag (p. 126). WIN! And, well, personally, I think it's a real shame to iron or treat your entrelac in some way when you have finished it. Ironing can make it look really flat and ruin the woven effect. But it's up to you, of course.

Instructions

Bit by Bit Pillow

Another of Lulu's absolutely wonderful drawings.

Basic yarn ★ 2 strands Peruvian Highland Wool together, 1 strand Fritidsgarn alone, 1 strand Brushed Alpaca plus 1 strand Tilia or Arwetta, 1 strand Cloud plus 1 strand Tilia or Arwetta, 1 strand Phoenix plus 1 strand Peruvian Highland Wool (Yarn types and alternatives, p. 254).

Scrap yarn ★ Lots of balls, skeins and threads for knitting squares. Varying lengths of thick, thin, smooth and shaggy yarns, wound to balls or skeins (p. 234). Knit with 1, 2, 3 or 4 strands simultaneously – or even more if you like.

Size ★ Approx. 40 x 40 cm when cushion is inside case.

Yarn requirement ★ At least 200 g in total.

Needles ★ Circular needle size 7, 60-80 cm (this item is knitted in rows), crochet hook size 7 (for assembly).

Materials ★ Cushion 40 x 40 cm, available almost everywhere to buy new or second hand. If it's second hand, sniff it. I speak from experience.

Tension square ★ Approx. 12 sts and 14-17 rows St st with needles size 7 = 10 x 10 cm. (Tension, p. 239, Tension in entrelac, p. 171) If your gauge is different, use thicker or thinner needles.

Knit an entrelac cushion cover! It's going to be awesome! I have finally come to accept the cushion as a legitimate designer object. Officially, at least. I recommend trying entrelac knitting on a cushion first as it's a good idea to try out colours, techniques, yarns and materials on a project that's not too much of a commitment. I can't stand knitting swatches that end up in a drawer. It's a waste of good yarn and valuable knitting time. So a cushion is perfect! Get all those ideas that you have in your head – good, bad or ugly – out there and onto your cushion. By the time you've finished, you will virtually have a PhD in entrelac, I promise you. If you can't handle the cushion, turn to p. 192 and do a Barbie Knit instead.

The cushion cover is knitted in 2 "identical" parts which you then crochet together with double crochets. You can add some tassels at the end. Pure rock'n'roll. This cushion is 3 squares across, each square being 10 stitches. So, it's 30 stitches in total, just like in the intro to entrelac on p. 163. For cushions, I prefer slightly rougher, denser stitches. That way, it will take you several nursery rhymes and more telly to knit.

>

A McChicken with cheese, big menu with fries, mineral water, Béarnaise dip, seven chilli-cheese toppings ... No, wait, can I make 15 out of that...?

MOR
MOR
MOR

Beige goes with everything. End of!

Basic instructions

Front and back ★ Cast on 30 sts using needle size 7 and random yarn. Knit first tier of half-squares according to instructions (p. 165). Knit a tier of right-leaning half and full-squares (p. 165). Then knit a tier of left-leaning squares (p. 168), a tier of right-leaning squares, then another tier of left- and another tier of right-leaning squares. Finish with a row of left-leaning half-squares (p. 160). Voilà! One side of the cushion done!

Knit the other side in exactly the same way. With different colours, techniques and yarns, maybe?

You now have two same-sized pieces. More or less. If they are not quite the same size, no worries. That can happen if your change yarn or technique. Nothing I've ever knitted has been the same size. Ever.

Assembly ★ Sew in or knot the ends. You are now going to crochet the two cushion panels together around their four edges. Lay the two pieces on top of each other, WS together, so that the half-squares and the cast-on edges meet. That will look best. To crochet the pieces together, use a firm yarn you like to work with, e.g. 2 strands Peruvian Highland Wool (p. 254). Starting at any corner and with hook size 7, crochet the first of the four sides together with double crochets (p. 244). Push the hook through both loops of the BUTT (p. 248). Don't crochet too loosely, nor too tightly. You know the drill. It's when you crochet the parts together like this that the BUTT really comes into its own. The number of sts per half-square should be the same on each panel. If it's not, try and make it match somehow. It's easiest to keep an eye on the half-squares. Keep track of how many you have already crocheted together rather how many are still to go.

At each corner, do 3-4 double crochets through both loops of the corner stitch. If you can't quite see which is the corner stitch, just poke into where it looks like there might be a hole. That will give you a nice, rounded corner. You might need three double crochets, you might need four. Just try it out and see what looks best. Crochet the next side seam together in the same way. And then the third. You have now crocheted the seams on three of the four sides. If it takes a while to get the double crochets, corners and edges more generally to look good, take the time you need. It will be worth it in the end.

Before crocheting the fourth side seam together in the same way as you did the other three, put the cushion into the cover and flatten it, pushing the corners neatly into the corners of the cover. When you have crocheted the last corner, cut off the thread, do a good old slip stitch into the first double crochet, pull the thread all the way through and give it a good tug. Using your crochet hook, pull the thread into the cushion and back out the front. Pull it slightly, then cut it off and leave to disappear back into the inside of the cushion cover.

You'll know from my first book how much I love cushions in general – especially knitted ones.

Instructions

Bit by Bit Cardy/Sweater (grownups)

I'm damn proud of this one! A floor-length entrelac coat in beige. I started knitting it when my dad died. So much for facing up to your demons.

Basic yarn ★ 1 strand Peruvian Highland Wool alone, 1 strand Fritidsgarn alone, 1 strand Brushed Alpaca alone, 1 strand Cloud alone, 3 strands Tilia or 3 strands Arwetta together (Yarn types and alternatives, p. 254).

Scrap yarn ★ Varying lengths of thick, thin, smooth and shaggy yarns, wound to balls or skeins (p. 234). Knit with 1, 2, 3 or 4 strands simultaneously - or even more if you like.

Size ★ 1-2 (3-4) 5-6 (7-8) (Size guide, p. 239).

Chest measurement of garment ★ Approx. 120 (130) 140 (150) cm. This measurement is the total circumference measured just under the armhole of the pullover. Remember: this number is just a rough guide. Wink, wink. Also, this sweater only comes in four sizes as it's oversized.

Total length ★ The more tiers of squares you knit, the longer the garment will be. Simple logic. Hold the back up to yourself in front of the mirror to check the length. Add another two tiers of squares if you want it longer. Always make fronts the same length as backs. If you want to add ribbing to the bottom, bear in mind that it will make the garment longer, as you will add it at the end.

Yarn requirement ★ Approx. 3 balls Peruvian Highland Wool for ribbing. And as for the rest, it's impossible to say. To find out why, turn to p. 250.

Needles ★ Circular needle size 6, 80-100 cm (for sleeves, front(s) and back, knitted in rows), circular needle size 5.5, 60-80 cm (for ribbing and neck), crochet hook size 6 (for assembly and, if desired, edging).

Tension square ★ Approx. 14 sts and 16-19 rows garter st with needle size 6 = 10 x 10 cm. (Tension, p. 239, Tension in entrelac, p. 171) If your gauge is different, use thicker or thinner needles.

Entrelac is great to knit. It really is. But have you tried knitting a sample yet (p. 163)? I recommend starting with a small one.

This is an oversized design and slightly 80s. The sweater has a wonderful V-neck. Use the yarns you have lying around in the colours that you like. If necessary, buy a few additional balls to match. Individual squares made with novelty or colour-gradient yarns look great, by the way. Make a cardy or a sweater. Knit it short, in the classic length or really long. But remember: a long one will get longer with time as it drops under its own weight. So knit it 10-15 cm shorter than you ultimately want it to be.

This garment is made in the same way as the cushion (p. 174), i.e. all the pieces are knitted in rows and then crocheted together. But don't let that put you off – because with BUTT stitches on the edges, crocheting the pieces together is easy, pretty quick and great fun to do. Whether you want ribbing at the bottom of the sleeves is for you to decide. It looks good with or without.

>

True! This one turned out a bit short. But having just knitted the coat, I just couldn't handle any more. You can just knit yours longer if you like.

With this design, the pullover is five squares across on the front and back, and the cardigan is 2 squares across on each front and 5 across on the back. With each size up, each square is knitted one stitch wider. The sleeves are knitted in the same technique and are 4 squares across on both the cardy and the pullover. I think it's good to cast on every part, i.e. the back, front(s) and sleeves, in the same yarn. You could also use the casting-on yarn for the ribbing, perhaps. By casting on in the same yarn each time, you will always know which side is up. And it looks even more amazing if you use it to crochet the pieces together as well, as it gives the garment a kind of theme amid all the chaos.

Basic instructions

Back (sweater and cardy) ★ Cast on 50 (55) 60 (65) sts using circular needle size 6. Knit each half-square (and then each square) over 10 (11) 12 (13) sts. Work first tier of half-squares (p. 165). Don't forget to adapt the number of sts per square to suit the size you are making, of course. Turn. Work tier of right-leaning squares (p. 165). Turn. Work tier of left-leaning squares (p. 168). Turn. Now keep adding a tier of right-leaning squares followed by a tier of left-leaning ones until work is desired length (minus the final tier of half-squares and ribbing, if you are adding any). Your last tier of full squares will be right-leaning. Now finish with a tier of left-leaning half-squares (p. 169). The back is now done.

Front with V-neck (sweater) ★ Front and back must be same length and width. Work the front in exactly the same way as the back until you get to the neck. Start shaping the neck after a tier of right-leaning squares. So, when the front is one tier of left-leaning, one of right-leaning and a final tier of half-squares shorter than the back, it's time to shape the neck (see photo).

This is done by *not* knitting the middle squares. Finish the two sides of the neck hole separately, with half-squares on the edges. Follow these steps:

Right neck › Work a tier of left-leaning squares, but complete only two squares (regardless of what size sweater you are making). Turn. Complete two sides of neck separately. Start with the "active" (i.e. right) side. Follow instructions for tier of right-leaning squares. Work final tier – but only the two half-squares you can actually knit, of course. Leave right neck and now complete left neck.

Left neck › Work with RS facing. Your last tier was right-leaning squares. Leave aside the first 10 (11) 12 (13) sts from the square below that you have on your needle. We'll come back to those later, when you knit the neck. Work a tier of left-leaning squares – 2 squares in total. Then follow instructions for a tier of right-leaning squares (1 half-, 1 full, 1 half-square). Work final tier of half-squares. The front is now finished. Put work aside. You might need a rest now...

Fronts (cardy) ★ You need to knit two identical fronts – at least in terms of length and width. Which yarn types and colours go together is for you to decide. Start with right front. Cast on 20 (22) 24 (26) sts using circular needle size 6. Work full and half-squares across 10 (11) 12 (13) sts, as for back. Work in entrelac as for back until front is same length. Personally, I like the cardy best without a neck shaping. But you might think differently. And rightly so. Any time. Work left front to same length and width.

Sleeves (sweater and cardy) ★ The sleeves are knitted in a rectangle shape (which you then crochet onto the front and back). They are worked over 4 squares, each with the same number of sts as the squares on the front and back. Cast on 40 (44) 48 (52) sts on circular needle size 6. Work in entrelac (p. 163), but remember to use the right number of sts per square for the size you are knitting. How long to make the sleeves is entirely up to you, of course. Extra-long, impractical sleeves can look just as great as normal or three-quarter-length ones. The numbers of tiers required for the different sleeve lengths (excluding ribbing) are as follows:

Extra-long, totally impractical sleeves ★ One starting tier, three tiers each of right- and left-leaning squares, one tier of right-leaning squares, final tier.

Normal-length sleeves ★ One starting tier, two tiers each of right- and left-leaning squares, one tier of right-leaning squares, final tier.

Three-quarter-length sleeves ★ One starting tier, one tier each of right- and left-leaning squares, one tier of right-leaning squares, final tier.

Two identical sleeves. Fine. The sleeves are knitted in exactly the same way (although potentially with different yarns and colours). That means you get to choose which side of the sleeves will be the front. I always choose the nicest side. I'm not quite so bothered about the backs of the sleeves because I can't see them anyway.

A note on finishing and general tips on entrelac: As I said, neat edges are a must on this design, and you really notice it most when finishing the garment. The half and full squares should always finish flush (see photo on p. 163). There's a lot to work through now, which can be overwhelming, but the trick is to go at it step by step and think only about what to do next. It's a lot like grieving or getting to grips with other difficult situations we have to handle in life. Whatever you do, don't think it all has to be done in one go. Instead, do it in stages. Things always seem more terrifying beforehand than they actually are in the end. My mother had a friend who used to say: "Why worry beforehand? It just means you worry twice about the same thing." Anyway, crochet the pieces together in the following order: close the shoulder seams, attach the sleeves to the front and back, and then close the side and sleeve seams all in one go. Done.

Assembly (sweater and cardigan) ★ Use a size 6 crochet hook. Lay the back and front(s) on top of each other, with the wrong sides facing each other. With the pullover, the edges will be in line with each other all the way round. With the cardigan, you will need to place the fronts so that the shoulders lie on top of the shoulders of the back. This will leave a gap between the two fronts. Make sure the cast-on edges are at the bottom on all the pieces.

>

Picking up stitches for the neck.

With RS of sweater/cardy pieces facing outwards, use crochet hook size 6 and your casting-on yarn to close shoulder seams in slip st (p. 244). *Right shoulder* › Start seam on outside of right shoulder and work in towards neck. Align half-squares of front and back. For medium to short garment, crochet only through outer loop so the seam doesn't come out too bulky. For medium to long garment, crochet through both loops so that the shoulders are strong enough to hold the extra weight. Crochet neither too tightly nor too loosely, until all sts of front have been used. Cut off yarn. *Left shoulder* › Again, work with front facing you. Count sts on cast-off edge of front, then count same number of sts on back. That should be easy, as the squares are (more or less) aligned. Start from neck and crochet out to edge of shoulder as before, until all sts of front have been used. Cut off yarn. You now have two seams that go in the same direction and are simply beautiful. If your squares don't align completely (one might have 12 sts and the other 13 – it can happen!), don't worry. Just crochet 2 sts together or choose a stitch as a new stitch so everything fits. As Tim Gunn from Project Runway once said: "Make it work." Finish sleeves in same way. Spread assembled front(s) and back out in front of you, position (cast-off edge of) sleeve so shoulder seam is in middle, with 2 half-squares on either side of it = 4 squares in total for sleeve. Sleeve squares should align with 4 squares on each side of shoulder on front(s) and back. Crochet sleeves on using same yarn as before, by pushing hook through outer (or both, see above) loops. Repeat for second sleeve. With RS facing outwards, close side and sleeve seams by crocheting into outer (or both) loops of BUTT. Make sure your squares are aligned. Crochet neither too tightly nor too loosely – it's all about getting the balance right. Start one side seam on cuff and work up sleeve and along one side of back down to bottom edge. Start the other side seam on bottom edge of back and finish on cuff. That will give you a nice, symmetrical look, with the seams all going in the same direction. Sew in or knot the gazillions of ends.

V-neck (sweater) ★ Start from middle of back, RS facing. With circular needle size 5.5 and possibly your casting-on yarn, pick up 2 sts knitwise from each st and row of neck hole (i.e. from cast-off edge at back and BUTTS on sides). That means picking up sts from both the inner and outer loops of the BUTT. You can also use just the outer loop, which will automatically give you half the number of sts and a tighter, less deep neck. It depends what you prefer. Pick up sts along side of neck hole. Count how many you have picked up, and ensure same number on other side of middle st: when you get to middle of neck hole (i.e. to bottom of V), pick up 1 additional st and mark as middle st. Now work sts from stitch holder as they come: if picking up sts from outer loop only, work sts as they are. If picking up sts from both loops of BUTT, inc 1 on each st from stitch holder with tbl (p. 244) to get double the number of sts. Work both sides of neck in same way until you have same number of sts on each side and sts all the way around neck edge. I won't tell you the exact number of sts needed, as I think it's more important that you check your work yourself instead of thinking too hard about the numbers.

Knit a texture into some of the squares if you like (p. 205).

>

SILVAN
GØR-DET-SELV

Adding fringes (p. 214).

A few threads left dangling can look good too.

You may find you have a slightly different number of stitches from me. Work in rib (k1 tbl, p1) until one st before middle st. Slip next stitch along with middle st. Slip 2 st tog knitwise loosely, k1, pass 2 slipped sts over just-knitted st. You have now completed your first V-neck decrease. The st immediately after dec should be same as st before it. Sounds cryptic, but it basically just means that if you k before dec, k straight after it too. If you p before dec, p after it as well, of course. Rep dec in every rnd. Work a total of 6-8 rnds until everything looks nice and balanced. Now cast off all sts in rib (k above k, p above p), neither too tightly nor too loosely.

Ribbing/crocheted edge (at bottom and on sleeves) ★ To rib or not to rib? You decide. Both look good. Adding ribbing will give you a neater, more complete (and mature) look. Without, the cardy/sweater will look rougher. Either way, here's how to add ribbing to the bottom edge if you want to: *Sweater* › With circular needle size 5.5 and possibly your casting-on yarn, pick up 1 st from each st of cast-on edge. This will give you 100 (110) 120 (130) in total. Make sure you have an even number of sts. A few sts more or less are no problem. Work ribbing (k1 tbl, p1) to desired length, cast off in rib (k above k, p above p).

Personally, I don't think ribbing is needed around the bottom of a cardy. Quite the opposite, in fact: it seems a pity to cramp a cardy like that. A cardy is wild, baggy, free and different. So, let it be those things. Many of us are all those things ourselves. Instead of adding ribbing, one idea might be to add one, two or several rounds of double crochets all around the outside edge of the cardy. Start somewhere like the bottom of the side seam of the right front. Using a size 6 hook and your casting-on yarn, do a round of double crochets, pushing the hook through both loops of the BUTT edge stitches: crochet across the back to the far edge of the left front. At the corner, do 3-4 double crochets into the corner stitch and then work your way up the front left edge, round the neck and all the way back down to where you started, as it were. At every corner or rounded edge, do 3-4 double crochets into the corner stitch. Crochet a few rounds – or stop after just one if you prefer. If you like, add a few rounds of double crochets to the ends of the sleeves as well, if you are not adding ribbing.

Cuffs ★ With circular needle size 5.5 and possibly your casting-on yarn, pick up 3 sts for every 4 sts on cast-on edge = approx 30 (33) 36 (39) sts in total. You may have slightly more or less, but you need an even number. Work ribbing (k1 tbl, p1) to desired length, cast off in rib (k above k, p above p). Sew in or knot the ends.

Ribbing or not!

Instructions

Bit by Bit Cardy/Sweater (kids)

She chose the colours herself. Excellent choice, I reckon!

Basic yarn ★ 1 strand Peruvian Highland Wool alone, 1 strand Fritidsgarn alone, 1 strand Brushed Alpaca alone, 1 strand Cloud alone, 3 strands Tilia or 3 strands Arwetta together (Yarn types and alternatives, p. 254).

Scrap yarn ★ Lots of balls, skeins and threads for knitting squares. Varying lengths of thick, thin, smooth and shaggy yarns, wound to balls or skeins (p. 234). Knit with 1, 2, 3 or 4 strands simultaneously - or even more if you like.

Size ★ 2-4 (6-8) 10-12 years (Size guide, p. 239).

Chest measurement of garment ★ Approx. 68 (88) 98 cm. This measurement is the total circumference measured just under the armhole of the pullover.

Total length ★ Impossible to say. The more tiers of squares you knit, the longer it will be. If necessary, adapt length of back to match length of child's back. Add another two tiers of squares if you want it longer. Always make fronts the same length as backs. If you want to add ribbing to the bottom, bear in mind that it will make the garment longer, as you will add it at the end.

Yarn requirement ★ Approx. 2 balls Peruvian Highland Wool for ribbing. You will need less of the other yarns than for the grownups' *Bit by Bit* but more than for the Barbie version (p. 192) (Yarn requirements, p. 250)

Needles ★ Circular needle size 6, 80-100 cm (for sleeves, front and back, knitted in rows), circular needle size 5.5, 60-80 cm (for ribbing and neck), crochet hook size 6 (for assembly and, if desired, edging).

Tension square ★ Approx. 14 sts and 16-19 rows garter st with needle size 6 = 10 x 10 cm. (Tension, p. 239, Tension in entrelac, p. 171) If your gauge is different, use thicker or thinner needles.

With a few exceptions (e.g. the finishing on the sleeves and neck), the kiddies' *Bit by Bit Cardy/ Sweater* is knitted in exactly the same way as the grownups' – but with fewer stitches and squares, of course. Making it together with the child is fun. My daughter, Lulu, chose her favourite colours and yarns for this, and my job was to combine them. As far as colours and materials are concerned, children are refreshingly open to all the options. We grownups could learn a thing or two from them. It's wonderfully inspiring (with no strings attached) to be guided by a kid's curiosity and creativity. I discover new possibilities and combinations every time. It's an absolute gift.

The kids' version of the *Bit by Bit Cardy/ Sweater* comes in just three sizes, so check the child's chest measurement. In addition, read the info accompanying the grownups' version (p. 178). Once again, the ribbing is optional on this design, but I speak from experience when I recommend ribbing for the smallest sizes. Just in terms of home-made knits, wide sleeves, and bread and jam. Better safe than sorry.

NEW YOR
BALENCIAGA

Basic instructions

Back (sweater and cardy) ★ Cast on 33 (36) 39 sts on circular needle size 6. Knit each half-square (and then each square) over 11 (12) 13 sts. Work first tier of half-squares (p. 165). Don't forget to adapt the number of sts per square to suit the size you are knitting, of course. Turn. Work tier of right-leaning squares (p. 165). Turn. Work tier of left-leaning squares (p. 168). Turn. Now keep adding a tier of right-leaning squares followed by a tier of left-leaning ones until work is desired length (minus the final tier of half-squares and ribbing, if you are adding any). Your last tier of full squares will be right-leaning. Now finish with a tier of left-leaning half-squares (p. 169). The back is now done. For a classic-length sweater, a good option is: one starting tier, two tiers each of right- and left-leaning squares, one more tier of right-leaning squares, one final tier. Adapt as needed.

Front with V-neck (sweater) ★ Front and back must be same length and width. So, work the front in exactly the same way as the back until you get to the neck. Start shaping the neck after a tier of right-leaning squares. When the front is one tier of left-leaning, one of right-leaning and a final tier of half-squares shorter than the back, it's time to shape the neck (see photo). This is done by *not* knitting the middle squares. Finish the two sides of the neck hole separately, with half-squares on the outside edges. Confused? Follow these steps: *Right neck* › Work as for a tier of left-leaning squares, but complete only 1 square (for all sizes). Turn. Complete each side of neck separately. Start with the "active" (i.e. right) side. Follow instructions for tier of right-leaning squares. Knit 2 half-squares in total. Work final tier – but only the half-square you can actually knit, of course. Leave right neck and now complete left neck. *Left neck* › Work with RS facing. Your last tier was right-leaning squares. Place the first 11 (12) 13 sts from the square below on a stitch holder. We'll come back to those later, when you knit the V-neck. Work a tier of left-leaning squares – 1 square in total. Then follow instructions for tier of right-leaning squares (2 half-squares in total). Work final tier. The front is now finished. Put aside.

Fronts (cardy) ★ You need to knit two identical fronts – at least in terms of length and width. Start with right front. Cast on 11 (12) 13 sts on circular needle size 6. As with back, work full and half-squares across 11 (12) 13 sts. The front is just one square wide. Work in entrelac until front is exactly same length as back. Personally, I like the cardy best without a neck shaping. Work left front to same length and width.

Sleeves ★ The sleeves are knitted in a rectangle shape (which you then crochet onto the front and back). They are worked over 3 squares, each with the same number of sts as the squares on the front and back. Cast on 33 (36) 39 sts on circular needle size 6. Work in entrelac (p. 163), but remember to use the right number of sts per square for the size you are knitting. For the kids' version I recommend either normal or three-quarter-length sleeves.

Normal-length sleeves ★ One starting tier, two tiers each of right- and left-leaning squares, one tier of right-leaning squares, final tier.

Three-quarter-length sleeves ★ One starting tier, one tier each of right- and left-leaning squares, one tier of right-leaning squares, final tier.

Knit two identical sleeves.

Assembly (sweater and cardy) ★ Order of assembly: Close shoulder seams, attach sleeves to front(s) and back, close side and sleeve seams all in one go. Tadaaah!

Here's how it's done › *Crochet hook size 6 (for assembly).* Lay back and front(s) with wrong sides facing towards each other. With the pullover, the edges will align all the way round. With the cardy, lay the fronts so that the shoulders align with the shoulders of the back.

Crochet the triangles on the shoulders and sleeves together in an "staggered" arrangement – unlike with *Bit by Bit* for grownups (p. 178), where they are aligned.

This will produce a gap down the middle of the front. Make sure the cast-on edges are at the bottom of all pieces. With RS of sweater/cardy pieces facing outwards, using crochet hook size 6 and casting-on yarn, close shoulder seams in slip st (p. 244). *Right shoulder* › Start seam on outside of right shoulder. Align half-squares of front and back. For medium or short garment, crochet only through outer loop so the seam doesn't come out too bulky. Crochet neither too tightly nor too loosely, until all sts of front have been used. Cut off yarn. *Left shoulder* › Again, work with RS facing. Count sts on cast-off edge of front, then count same number of sts on back. That should be easy, as the squares are (more or less) aligned. Start from neck and crochet as before, until all sts of front have been used. Cut off yarn. You now have two seams that go in the same direction and are simply beautiful. If your squares don't align completely (one might have 12 sts and the other 13 – it can happen!), don't worry. Just crochet 2 sts together or choose a st to make a new st so everything fits together.

The sleeves on the kids' version are finished slightly differently to the grownups'. On the kids' version, for practical reasons, the sleeves are slightly narrower. This means the squares of the front(s) and back will align with half-squares on the sleeves when you crochet them together (see photo) Here's how it's done: Spread out assembled front(s) and back in front of you, position (cast-off edge of) sleeve so shoulder seam is in middle of it and there are 1.5 half-squares on either side of seam = 3 sleeve squares in total. Position sleeve so that shoulder seam is in middle of centre sleeve square. Crochet sleeves on using casting-on yarn, by pushing hook through outer loops. Repeat for second sleeve. With RS facing outwards, close side and sleeve seams by crocheting into outer (or both) loops of BUTT – just as you did when assembling the front(s) and back. Make sure your squares are aligned. Work with crochet hook size 6 and casting-on yarn, crocheting neither too loosely nor too tightly. Start one side seam on cuff, then work down along one side of back to bottom edge. Start the other side seam on bottom edge of back and finish on cuff. That will give you a nice, symmetrical look, with the seams all going in the same direction. Sew in or knot the gazillions of ends.

>

I knitted part of this with an old scarf, which I had cut into strips beforehand. (For more on fabrics and ribbons, see p. 208)

V-neck (sweater) ★ Start from middle of back, RS facing. With circular needle size 5.5 and possibly your casting-on yarn, pick up 1 st knitwise from each st/row of neck hole (from cast-off edge at back and BUTTS on sides). With the kids' sweater it doesn't look cool if the neck is too big, so pick up just 1 st per st/row. Pick up sts along side of neck hole. Count how many you have picked up, and ensure same number on other side of middle st: when you get to middle of neck hole (i.e. to bottom of V), pick up 1 additional st and mark as middle st. Now work sts from stitch holder as they come.

Work round left and right sides of neck hole until you have same number of sts on each side. I won't tell you the exact number of sts needed, as I think it's more important that you check your work yourself instead of thinking too hard about the numbers. You may have few sts more or less than me. Continue in rib (k1 tbl, p1) until 1 st before middle st. Slip 2 st tog knitwise loosely, k1, pass 2 slipped sts over just-knitted st. You have now made your first V-neck decrease. Work st straight after dec in same way as st right before dec. Sounds cryptic but it basically means: if you k1 before dec, k1 after it too. If you p1 before it, then p1 after it. Rep on every rnd. Work a total of 5-7 rnds until the overall effect looks neat and in proportion. Cast off in rib (k above k, p above p), not too tightly, not too loosely.

Ribbing/crocheted edge (at bottom edge and on sleeves) sweater ★ With circular needle size 5.5 and casting-on yarn, pick up 1 st from each st of cast-on edge. This will give you 66 (72) 78 sts in total. Make sure you have an even number of sts. A few sts more or less are no problem. Work ribbing (k1 tbl, p1) to desired length, cast off in rib (k above k, p above p). Instead of ribbing, you can also finish the bottom edge of the cardy with 1, 2 or more rows of double crochets (see grownups' version p. 185, follow instructions under "Ribbing/crocheted edge").

Cuffs ★ With circular needle size 5.5 and casting-on yarn, pick up 3 sts for every 4 sts on cast-on edge = approx 24 (26) 28 sts in total. You may have slightly more or less, but you need an even number. Work ribbing (k1 tbl, p1) to desired length, cast off in rib (k above k, p above p). Sew in or knot the ends.

The BUTT: the edge stitch that will set you free.

Barbie Knit

Bit by Bit Sweater

Basic yarn ★ 1 strand Arwetta alone, 3 strands Tilia together, 1 strand Mille Colori Baby alone. This knit is best done with yarns for needle size 3-3.5 mm (approx.). Other than that, mix and match as desired. (Yarn types and alternatives, p. 254)

Btw, cutting off the yarn and switching colour after every square really gets on my nerves, so I recommend just knotting the ends and switching wherever – or using a colour-gradient yarn like Mille Colori Baby.

Scrap yarn ★ Lots of balls, skeins and threads for knitting squares. Varying lengths of thick, thin, smooth and shaggy yarns, wound to balls or skeins (p. 234).

Size ★ One size.

Yarn requirement ★ At least 20 g.

Needles ★ Size 3.5 (It's up to you whether you use circular or straight needles to knit in rows), crochet hook size 3.5 (for assembly).

Pattern ★ Entrelac technique, see p. 163 for details.

Basic instructions

Front ★ Work in entrelac, as described on p. 163. Each square is 5 sts wide and you will need 3 squares across in total. *Here's how it's done* › Cast on 15 sts using needle size 3.5. Work first tier of 3 half-squares. Turn. Work 1 row of right-leaning full and half-squares. Turn. Work 1 row of left-leaning full squares. Turn. Work 1 row of right-leaning full and half-squares. Turn. Work 1 row of left-leaning full squares. Turn. Work 1 row of right-leaning full and half-squares. Turn. Finish with a row of left-leaning half-squares. Cut off yarn. Knit back in exactly the same way.

Sleeves ★ Work sleeves in entrelac, as for front and back, but with just 2 squares, each 5 sts across. *Here's how it's done* › Cast on 10 sts using needle size 3.5, work first tier of 2 half-squares. Turn. Work 1 tier of right-leaning full and half-squares. Turn. Work 1 tier of left-leaning full squares. Turn. Work 1 tier of right-leaning full and half-squares. Turn. Finish with a row of left-leaning half-squares. Cut off yarn. Knit second sleeve in exactly the same way.

Assembly ★ Assemble as described for Bit by Bit Cardy/Sweater, p. 181. With crochet hook size 3.5, first close right and left shoulder seams of front and back with approx. 5 double crochets (p. 244) each, so that the hole in the middle is big enough for Barbie/Ken's head and hair. Attach sleeves and close sleeve and side seams as described on p. 181. Knot the ends.

Why not just knit with a colour-gradient yarn? It will save you from all those ends – of which there are many!

Just tie knots babygirl

Chapter 5

Remember life and then your life becomes a better one ... unexpected help came from Lukas Graham.

thank you

After the funeral, life returned to normal pretty quickly: taking Lulu to childcare, going to work, answering emails, eating spag bol and watching *Real Housewives*. From the outside everything was normal, but on the inside it wasn't. I just wasn't really there. I don't know where I was, but I definitely wasn't where everyone else was – or indeed where I had been myself before all this happened. It felt as though my dad had taken me with him.

Grownup Lærke was gone. All that remained was the little, insecure child that had always tried to do the right thing. For a very long time, he had been all-consuming, but with his death, it felt as though he had taken the last strong part of me with him. "You'll be fine. It just takes time," people said. "But when? And how?" I wondered. I felt trapped and didn't know how to get out.

I felt lonely and blamed myself. My life had become alien to me. I felt as though I was wrapped in plastic and experiencing everything through this transparent layer. I could see everything – but felt nothing. Not a hug, not even when I touched my own arm. I felt totally cut off, except as a mother to Lulu. She brought me to life. It was as though – through her – my dad and I had another chance.

I felt under terrible pressure from outside to hurry up and "get over it". At the funeral – and for a short while afterwards – I was allowed to be sad, but then I no longer felt I could give in to my grief. No one actually said that, but grief is an unwelcome guest, one that's unbearable to have around, that stays too long and eats up all your energy. I felt stuck. I was grieving not just because I had lost my father but because of our lost relationship and an entire life of misunderstandings, shame, guilt and accusations. His death was also a final farewell to something I had never had – and would never have. I had no control over my feelings. Fear would appear and I'd get aggressive. I was angry. I was absolutely furious – when I wasn't scared sh*tless. I was scared sh*tless of dying. And the fact that I was scared sh*tless made me furious.

Just as I had become a mother myself and was no longer all about just me, I witnessed how fast a healthy, strong individual can become weak and sick. I watched my father fade away. And watching someone die leads to the direct realisation that we all have to die at some point. No sh*t. I actually thought I would die too and developed an all-consuming fear of death. I thought I had cancer in my breast, my lung, my eyes, my legs, my teeth. I made my doctor

10,-
10,-

send me for a mammogram even though she knew full well I was just imagining it all. I had all my moles and what-not double-checked too, until one day my doctor said to me: "Maybe we should consider some other options. Therapy, perhaps, or a self-help group for the bereaved." Yes, I liked that idea. And with that, the first step was taken.

I had heard that Lukas Forchhammer from the band Lukas Graham had just lost his father around that time too, and I know it sounds creepy, but I almost felt as though I knew him a little. I grew up with the *The Crumbs* films starring him as the younger brother, Grunk. He had always been a constant in my life. I was just desperate to get out of my plastic wrapping and not feel alone anymore.

I read that Lukas Forchhammer wrote the song *7 Years.* One day, when I was alone in my studio, I put it on while knitting countless entrelac squares. It tells the story of a life, from childhood to adulthood, including birth, death, being someone's child and becoming a parent yourself. It's about giving and losing life, about the cycle of life, with yourself, your kids and their kids. And *you* have to carry on living, because there are cool things in life too and everything is possible. All you have to do is give it a go. So, there I was, sitting in my studio and listening to this song over and over again while knitting squares and contemplating life and death. As I listened, I wept – and knitted more and more squares.

Soon, I'll be 60 years old, my daddy got 61. Remember life and then your life becomes a better one.

"Remember life and then your life becomes a better one." Banal? Makes sense? A cliché? Who cares! Because those words were as important to me back then as they are now. I felt I had a duty to carry on living and to feel, touch, love, eat, kiss, smile, hug and knit. Incidentally, my dad was 61 too when he died.

I actually wrote a letter to Lukas because I felt this tremendous need to speak to someone who I thought would understand me. I wrote about my feelings as though to get closure on my relationship with my dad. I spent a long time trying to find out the address of Lukas Graham's manager – I needed a recipient to send my letter to. In fact, I spent so long trying to get it that in the meantime, fortunately, I realised my letter had actually been for my dad (and myself), not for Lukas. I didn't want to burden him with my grief: he had his own grief to be dealing with. Today I'm glad I kept the letter. It's proof of how much I loved my dad.

I listened to the Lukas Graham song every day for at least six months. It helped me realise that, with or without me, life goes on. After a long period of passivity, I started to get more active again. At the same time, I started thinking about my own story and all the things I was carrying around in me. It was all a part of me. And so was the grief. It made me stronger. I wasn't weak, like I had always thought. All the difficult things are just as much a part of me as the good ones. My grief was negative energy that already existed within me and had been part of me – and that I could convert into positive energy.

The reason I was me was because I was the product of all my experiences, disappointments and realisations in life so far. ALL of them. So, there was no reason at all to hide away or conceal anything. Instead, I had to stand up straight and embrace my past and future. I was responsible for my future. But it felt not so much like a burden but more like the power of freedom carrying me forwards. I was gradually starting to feel things again.

As for my hands, they were desperate to feel something again. They were craving experiences and feelings, longing for materials, the sensory, the tactile. You know that feeling when you rub a piece of fabric, yarn or whatever between your fingertips? You feel it and work out its potential by touching it. You connect with it. And maybe you come up with more inspiration, or a few more thoughts, ideas?

Crap-box – to me, you are everything!

If not, try leaving the hustle and bustle of the outside world behind you and closing your eyes. Touch something. I felt and felt things and thought: "I'm back, baby!" In my studio I have boxes and boxes of material that I have accumulated over the years. I call them crap-boxes. They are just boxes of stuff, yarns, fabrics, stones, needles, odds and ends – all sorts of crap, basically, that I thought was valuable at some point, for some reason or other. Valuable to me. My crap-boxes are the sum of myself. The sensuousness that makes me who I am. If you don't have a box, get yourself one and start collecting all that precious crap that makes you who you are. The people you live with might hate your box. But you won't!

I started wanting to experiment again, to try things out and do some research. I discovered my courage to fail and created what I call a "soft opening" onto the new Lærke. I was no longer the person I had been before. I was living more. And I wanted much more. I could be bold and experiment at my own pace with my knitting needles, materials and textures. And I noticed that handicrafts gave me self-assurance and a new will to live, come what may. You could say I had always known that – but only really realised it when my dad died.

All my childhood, right through into my twenties, I had longed to hear my father tell me I was good enough. I had dreamed of him saying: "I'm so proud of you, Lærke." The only time he ever said that to me was two months before he died. He was in Rigshospitalet and I had brought him a prepaid card for his mobile. He was confused from all his medication – but also more gentle than before. It was as though a wall between us had disappeared.

We went for a short walk in the park nearby and sat on a bench right outside the window of the room where I had given birth to Lulu nine months earlier. It was one of those absurdities in life. Or perhaps a meaningful coincidence. For the first time in five years, my dad gave me a hug and said, laughing: "You really remind me of my grandmother. She never did as she was told either. Luckily. I'm so proud that you are who you are, Lærke. If only we had had a little more time together."

A moment later his mind had gone again, closed up, and he started chiding me for having washed his T-shirts wrong and bought him just one prepaid card and not two. Later, my mother told me that my father had loved and respected his grandmother more than anyone else in the family.

I felt as though I was standing on the bottom rung of a ladder and looking up. It was a long, steep climb. And that was how I experienced the grief after my dad died. But the first step is the hardest, and if Lukas could do it, then so could I. It felt like embarking on a huge, unmanageable knitting project where you know progress will be slow and arduous but you are still totally excited.

Closure between my dad and me is probably something I will never achieve. I know that now. He is dead. That's the way things turned out. But this book is my closure. And it's a closure I alone am responsible for – and one that I'm pretty damn proud of.

Experimenting and remixing the stuff in my crap-box helped me find my way back to myself. Maybe you want to try remixing your life and knitting too?

BTW

Hello Lukas,
Thank you so much for the song *7 Years.* It gave me the space to be with my father whenever I need to, without feeling guilt or shame. Without your song, I wouldn't be where I am now in my life.
Best

Lærke

Various beautiful textured patterns for the *Bit by Bit* kids' pullover, p. 186.

Remix your knits

This is where you get an exclusive glimpse of all the stuff in my crap-box and a bit of guidance on how to remix your knitting and nurture your creativity. These are just a few suggestions, so see them as the bottom rung on the longest and most fun ladder in the world – and gradually work your way up.

Knit and purl

Create textures with simple knit and purl stitches, and use them to decorate individual entrelac squares, for instance. Or convert Fair Isle charts into plain and purl instead of colours – although you need to be knitting in unicolour to do this. If you are working with multiple colours, things can get confusing!

Fair Isle patterns like houndstooth and stars are quite easy to translate into knit and purl. Instead of using two colours, just recreate the pattern in knit and purl stitches. Truly classy, huh? Simply done – à la Lærke Bagger. So, let me take you through that again, just to make it clearer:

Take a close look at your colour chart. To me it seems logical to do the coloured boxes so that they appear as purl stitches on the front of your work. The empty boxes will then appear as your knit stitches. But you can also do it the other way round.

If you are knitting in rows, proceed as follows: › When the right side of your work is facing you, purl the coloured-in boxes. When the wrong side of your work is facing you, do them in knit. If you are knitting in rounds, always do the coloured-in boxes in purl. Sound complicated? It isn't. Not at all. All you need to do is make sure you get the first few rows or rounds set up properly, with no mistakes.

But that's nothing new, is it? And of course, it's best to use light colours because that way the pattern stands out more.

When you do entrelac, you can make fantastic squares with all sorts of different textural patterns. It adds a wonderful "drama" to your knitting, and you won't get bored making it either. Crucially, though, you need to make sure you keep the edges nice, for instance by doing BUTT stitches (p. 242). That will give you the neatest finish on the edges where you pick up your stitches.

I have experimented with various types of knit-purl patterns, including different sizes of seed stitch, but essentially, there's no limit to what you can do. It's the same with cables, loops, Fair Isle patterns, bobbles, embroidery and so on.

Obviously, you will need to adapt your chosen pattern to suit the number of stitches you have. You might like to try it out by knitting a swatch. Personally, I don't think entrelac squares need to be perfect. After all, they are just a nice contrast to the plain stocking-stitch squares. But remember: the BUTT does not count as part of your pattern!

I used the following patterns:

- ★ **Reverse stocking stitch** › When the right side of your work is facing you, work all stitches in purl.
- ★ **Moss (seed) stitch** › Use an even number of sts. Row/round 1: k1, p1, rep to end of row/round. Row/round 2: p1, k1, rep to end of row/round.
- ★ **Moss stitch across 2 sts** › Use a multiple of four sts. Row/round 1: k2, p2, rep to end of row/round. Row/round 2: p2, k2, rep to end of row/round.

Other than that, I just used different variations on those three patterns. Basically, you can knit a hell of a lot of funky textures using nothing but plain and purl.

Other Fair Isle patterns

When it comes to Fair Isle patterns, the sky is the limit. Here are a few of my favourites, which you can use as borders, stripes or all-over, such as houndstooth on the *Fancy Cardy/Sweater* (p. 132). But remember: you always need two to four stitches in addition to your repeats as these will be your border stitches left and right.

If you are knitting a design that incorporates all different kinds of Fair Isle patterns – like the *Let It All Hang Out Scarf* on p. 218 – adapt the number of border stitches as needed to give you the right number of stitches for your pattern. So, for example, if your scarf is 36 stitches wide but your pattern is just 30 stitches wide, use the 3 spare stitches you have on either side as a border. Knit them in garter or stocking stitch, whichever you prefer. And if you find yourself getting itchy fingers, go to Pinterest and have a good look around there. You can also check out the old pegboard templates from your fuse beads, if you still have any around.

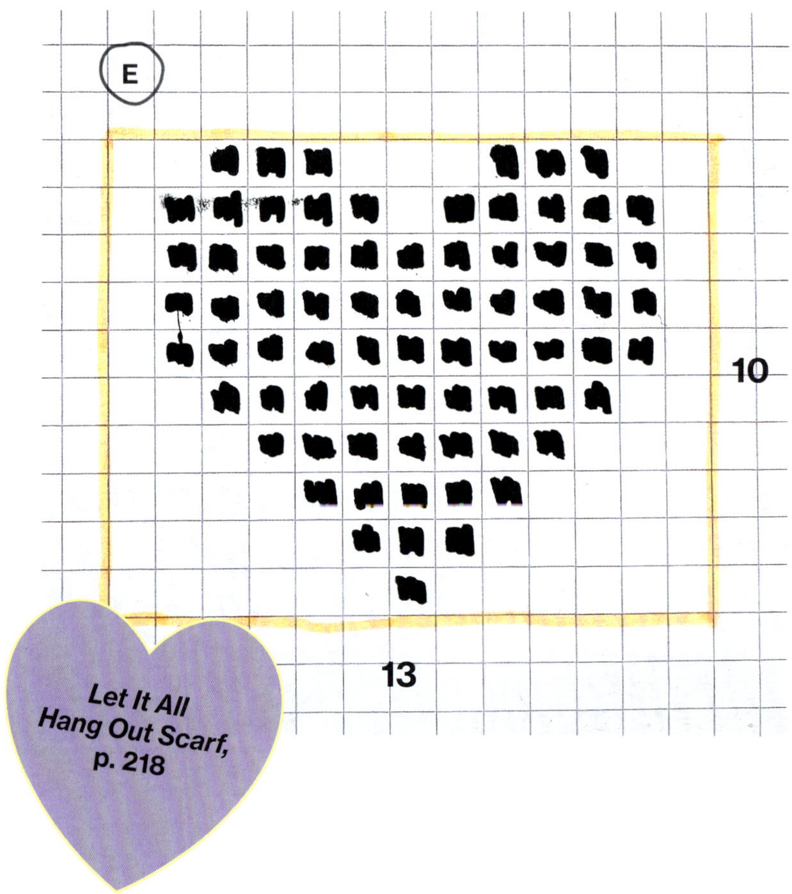

Additional colour charts for the *Let It All Hang Out Scarf* (p. 218) or the *Norske Genser* (p. 224).

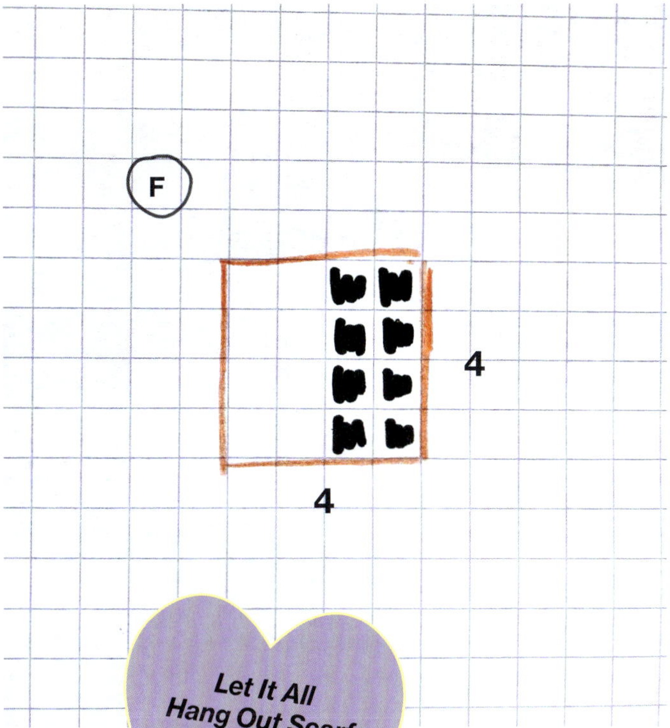

Let It All
Hang Out Scarf
(p. 218)

Tips on making your own Fair Isle colour charts

First of all, remember to include two or four additional stitches so you have a border along the left and right edges. Otherwise things could get ugly – and impossible to knit. To find out how many repeats and border stitches you will need, divide the total number of stitches on your scarf or pullover by the number of stitches in the repeat. If you end up with a number like 7.5, multiply the number of stitches across the repeat by – in this case – 7, and incorporate the remaining stitches evenly distributed into the borders on either side of your pattern.

It's easiest if you sketch your colour pattern onto squared paper. Sketch in the number of repeats you will need across your garment + the edge stitches. It's also a good idea to keep your sketches, for instance in a process book. That way you won't have to start from scratch if you ever want to do the pattern again.

Combine different types of yarn. In Fair Isle it looks awesome!

Count your stitches! At least on the first few rows. I never count mine and always end up regretting it because I have the wrong number – because I didn't count!

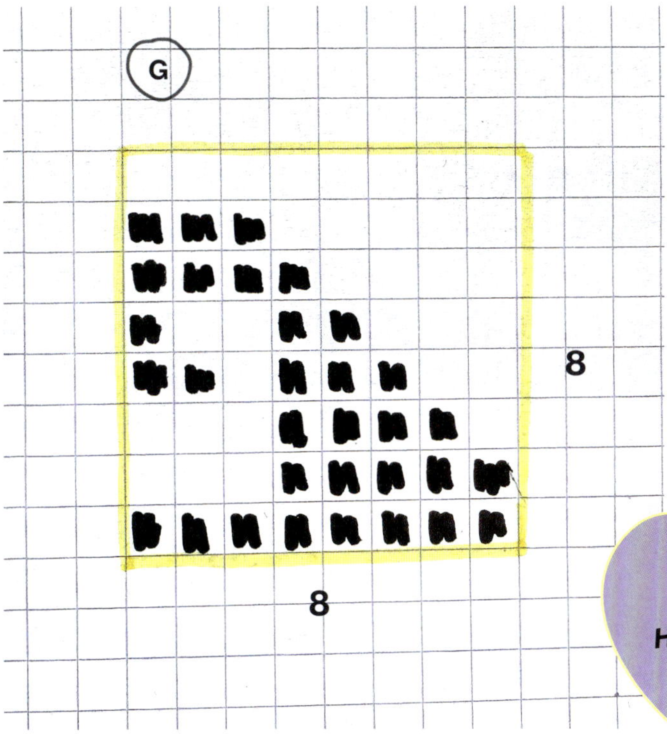

Relax, honey!

Let It All
Hang Out Scarf
(p. 218)

Ribbons and fabrics

Ribbons and fabrics make great novelty yarns and are a wonderful way to add cute special effects to your knitting. All you need to do is let go of the idea of creating something harmonious and beautiful. Ribbons and fabrics don't behave like yarns – and that's exactly what makes them so cool!

When I was a kid, I always used to keep the ribbons from gifts. Quite often, the beautiful wrapping with a fantastic bow was almost better than the actual gift! A few years ago I started collecting ribbons again and have been squirrelling away anything I can get my hands on ever since. It's such a waste to throw away perfectly good materials.

Use the ribbons and fabrics as yarns. Knot them in, leave the ends dangling, or knit individual strips of them into your work. They are also great for double-stranded work or for knitting double-stranded along with different pattern colours.

Ribbons are fairly similar to yarns, i.e. they are long and ready to use. Fabrics, on the other hand, have to be cut or torn into knittable strips first.

Large *Fancy Bag* (p. 126) in size 2 after felting. Don't worry about felting ribbons and fabrics along with the rest of your knit. They'll be fine – as long as your basic yarn is feltable.

Tips on using ribbons and fabrics

The easiest way to cut fabric is by laying it out on the table. You can also buy a cutter to help you. It's easier on the hands and quicker as well. But don't forget to lay something underneath to protect your table!

Cut a strip of fabric that roughly suits the needles you intend to use. A rough fit will do. Now knit a small sample – before you spend hours cutting strips the wrong width!

As you knit, take breaks in between because knitting fabrics can be tough on your hands and wrists, especially if you are using something hard like denim. If the strip is too wide and forms lumps when you knit it, cut a narrower one until it fits. You might find that a bit daft, but I think it makes it even nicer.

I have picked up all sorts of ribbon remnants lying around in department stores at Christmas. It really is incredible how often a piece of ribbon is cut to the wrong length and then just dumped in the bin. If you're lucky, you might be able to find a whole lot of stuff in the recycling bin too.

I collect not just ribbons but fabrics too: old clothes, for instance, kids' clothes, bed linen, curtains, tablecloths with holes or stains... A yucky old quilt cover that's covered in stains from being on a baby's bed deserves a new lease of life!

Ribbons and fabrics with logos look great too. For maximum impact, leave an end hanging out.

Go the whole hog and imagine all the possible alternative materials you could potentially knit with. Or almost all of them. But don't destroy anything that is still usable or even new. Recycle it or give it away instead.

If your fabric is cotton, it will be easy to tear into strips – which will save you a lot of time. Just cut a nick on the edge to start, and away you go.

And by the way › Don't try to make things look nice. A ribbon is not supposed to lie neat and flat, so don't try and turn your textile into something it isn't. Just let it be wild and completely itself.

Love,

Lærke

You can pick up all sorts of ribbon for free, believe me!

Sequins and holes in combination. This is a *3-Day Sweater* (p. 54) but without the yoke. Instead, I just cast off the body and sleeves and stitched them together under the arms.

Sequins (and beads)

When I was a kid, I used to love beads. I still do now, in fact. And over the last few years I have worked on integrating them into my knits. But then, oh man, I realised how much I love sequins as well – and how terribly I have neglected them! I find it really embarrassing to admit! When I was little, I remember sometimes being taken along to the Fredensborg Indkøbscentral shopping mall, before it became the Panduro, to choose something I liked. Often it was shimmering butterfly sequins because they were the most glittery. And what a joy it was when I found them again! I ran wild with them and had some truly great but also annoying experiences that I am happy to share with you here. If you just want to knit with beads, turn to p. 251.

Tips on knitting with sequins

Knitting with sequins is exactly the same as knitting with beads. All you do is thread them onto your yarn and pull them up one at a time whenever you want to knit one in (p. 251).

If your yarn is too thick to thread sequins onto (e.g. for the Let It All Hang Out Scarf on p. 218), thread them onto something thinner instead and knit that along with your main thread, double-stranded.

One of the cool things about knitting with sequins (and there are many more to come) is the fact that you can knit in far more of them than beads because they don't weigh much. You can also use big ones, no problem, to decorate finer, thinner knits. Very nice indeed.

I find medium and large sequins easiest to knit. The tiny ones can easily slip through to the back of your knitting – although that might also be a look you find you like. On a fine enough knit, it can look really great.

When you add a sequin, you might not always need to fix it in place by doing a twisted stitch above it, in the next row or round. The sequin might be so big that it can't actually slip from front to back. Just try it out and see what works.

Unlike beads, you can remove sequins from your knitting afterwards if you find you don't like them. If one has landed in a stupid place or perhaps doesn't fit in so well overall, just cut it out carefully with a sharp pair of scissors – but mind you don't cut through your yarn!

You can buy sequins wherever you can buy beads. And remember to share them with your kids – even if it is hard. I know. Alternatively, you can always hide them right up in the top of a cupboard.

Generally, sequins don't appreciate being washed in the machine, so you will need to wash your knits by hand, if you really feel they need it.

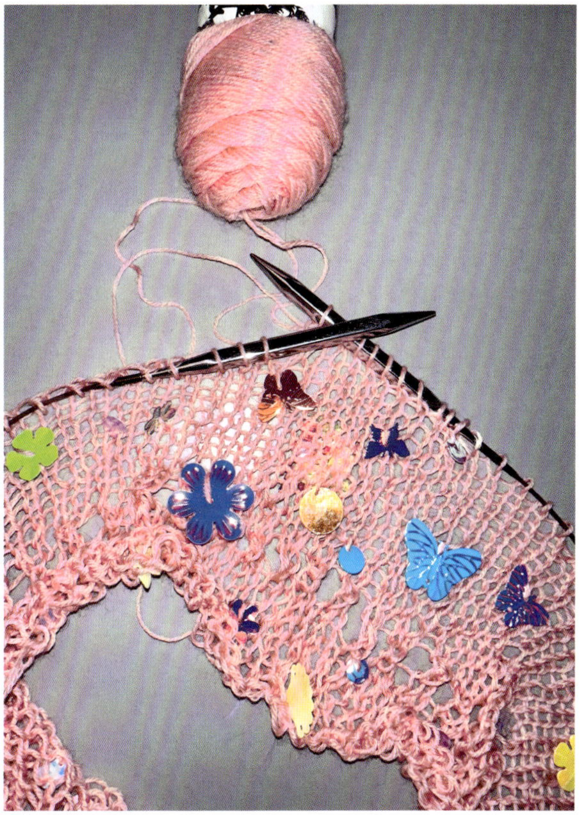

3-Day Sweater (p. 54) with sequins and holes. You can also make it with beads, provided they are not too heavy.

Special-effect yarns

Chenille, printed, sparkly, colour-gradient – you name it.

Yes, if there's one thing in knitting that's truly divisive, it's novelty yarns. You either love them, or you love to hate them. If you fall into the latter category, just skip the next section. If you're a true believer or undecided, carry on reading. Personally, I love them, of course, even if I do need a prolonged break from them from time to time. They can be too much of a good thing, you know.

Novelty yarns with special effects are one of the things I remember from growing up in the 1980s. My mother used to knit them, and I loved playing and fiddling around with them. I have been collecting novelty yarns for years and have a most enviable collection, though I say it myself. They are probably the only yarns in my stash that I'm stingy with. I tend to think something like: "Oooh, what a fabulous purple/green/turquoise/brown novelty yarn! Vintage 1987, I reckon..." When it comes to novelty yarns, I'm actually quite a connoisseur.

Tips on special-effect yarns

Use them, say, to add a special effect to your knit. Or go completely crazy and knit the entire thing out of novelty yarn. It will probably be quite sweaty to wear as most special-effect yarns are made of synthetic, so your skin can't breathe underneath them. Just saying. No judgement.

Cloud and Mille Colori Baby are fantastic new novelty yarns with colour gradients (p. 254). You'll often find novelty yarns in the recycling – leftovers from the 80s, when the trend was bigger than big. When you get them home, put them in the freezer for a while to kill off any creatures that might be living in them.

Novelty yarns are great for integrating into balls of scrap as individual strands from time to time. They add a really cool dynamic to your knitting. Entrelac squares in novelty yarns are really nice too. And fringes made with them look absolutely brilliant (p. 214).

Some novelty yarns can be a bit of a drag and irritating to knit. But if you add in a thinner yarn and knit the two together, double-stranded, you will find the novelty yarn slips better.

It actually took me longer to add the fringes to Barbie's coat (p. 146) than to the beige *Bit by Bit Cardy* (p. 178).

Fringes

Do you like your knitting to have that 90s cult feel too? Maybe you're obsessed with the film *Clueless*, where there are all those cardigans with fringes up them? Or might you just love fringes, like me? A bit of a fringe can look great on the cast-on edges of skirts, pullovers and cardigans. Or you can knot in a great big shaggy fringe all the way round so it looks like fur. You can also go completely bonkers and make an entire coat (!) out of fringes. With patterns, even! It will take you about 10,000 years to do, so don't say I didn't warn you...

Anyway, when it comes to fringes, anything goes. All you need is a pair of scissors, a crochet hook that's the same size as the needles you knitted the garment with, a piece of cardboard/plastic or a ruler, and a bit of yarn. Fringes are knotted in by what's called the Rya technique.

How to do fringes

The first thing you need to do is decide how thick you want the fringes to be. Do you want it thick and furry, or are you aiming for longer, thinner strands dangling down? The longer the threads are and the more fringes you add, the thicker and denser the result will be. Personally, I think it's a good idea to do a test section on your garment before you cut all your lengths of yarn. I would recommend lengths of between 12 and 28 cm. This will give you fringes between about 6 and 14 cm long, because when you have knotted them in, the strands will lie double.

Once you have decided how long your fringes will be, the next thing to do is take a rectangular piece of cardboard/plastic or a ruler or something solid that matches the length of your finished fringes. Now, wind the yarn around it. About 10-20 times will do for the moment, as you can always add more later on if you want.

Tips on fringes

When knotting in your fringes, it's easiest to work from bottom to top. That way, if you want layers of fringes, you won't end up working underneath the ones you have just knotted in.

Standing far enough away from your mirror, try the garment on to get more of an idea of what it will look like overall.

You can make fringes from any yarn, but the look will ultimately depend on what you have chosen. Chenille-type yarns create a thick, furry look. Cotton lies flatter. Phoenix and Brushed Alpaca are great for making fringes (p. 254).

If you want a thick, dense fringe, pull several threads through a stitch all in one go. That way it's quicker.

If your fringe is a bit uneven, you can fill any gaps by adding in individual threads here and there.

Cut your fringes into shape at the end if you want to.

Work your way through by adding your fringes gradually, symmetrically and systematically. That way, you will have more control over the way it looks (*Fancy Cardy*, p. 132).

And remember: it's OK to leave a bit out too!

Cut through the threads at one end to make them all the same length. Now knot the threads onto the horizontal bars between the stitches. You know me well enough by now not to be surprised when I say I can't tell you exactly how many or how thick your fringes should be. Just start somewhere, work your way up, and check your work as you go along. Is it turning out too loose? Or too tight, perhaps? Work symmetrically and systematically as you knot a thread onto each horizontal bar on each row between the stitches on both sleeves. Keep checking to see if you have enough and work your way up systematically.

If you're more the ride-or-die type, you can also cut some of the fringe threads to different lengths and knot them in. It will turn out great. But different.

1 Lay the threads for the fringe double and place them in the position you want. Push your crochet hook between the horizontal bars linking two stitches where you want to attach your fringe.

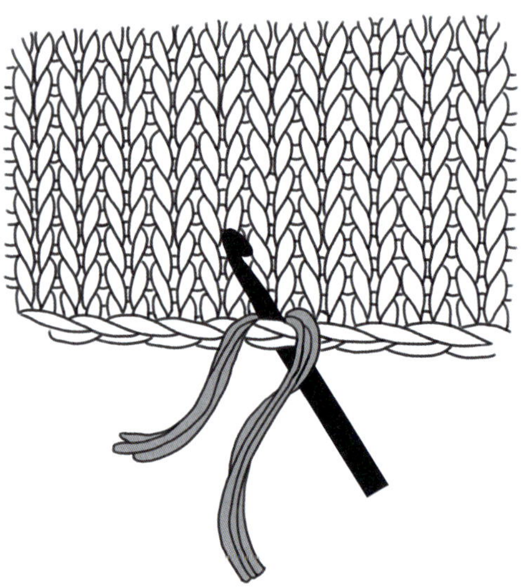

2 Using the hook, pull the threads through between the two stitches to create a loop.

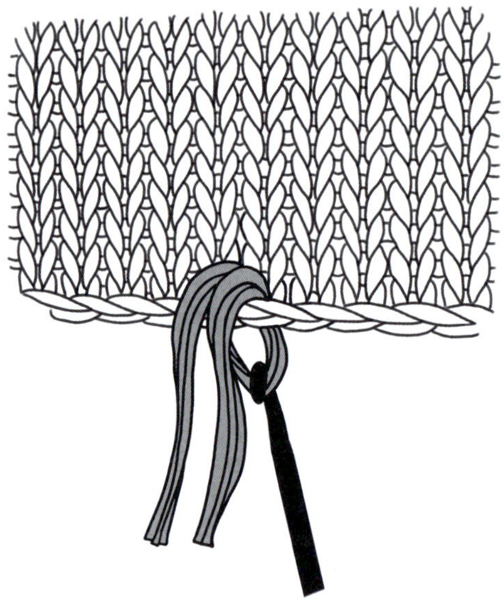

3 Now pull the threads through the loop and give them a gentle tug so that the fringe sits firmly on the knit.

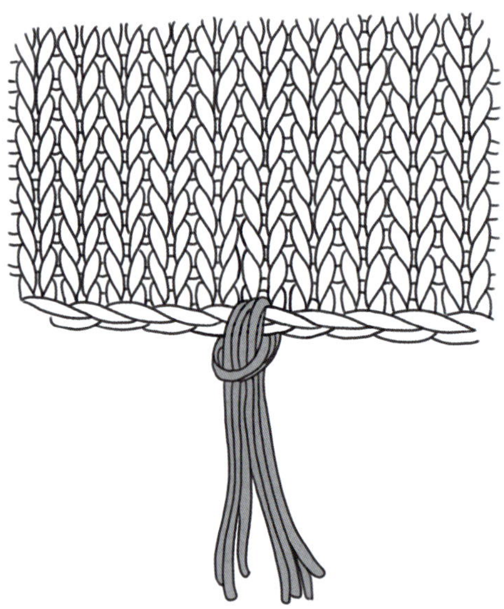

If you're more the ride-or-die type, you can also cut some of the fringe threads to different lengths and knot them in. It will turn out great. But different.

NEWSFLASH! *Handler Copenhagen* in Copenhagen has brilliant shoulder pads. Don't look at the price – they'll last you forever.

Shoulder pads

Yup, you read that right: shoulder pads! They're back! Finally! And really, nothing beats a pair of power shoulders in a neat little twinset, clingy knit or oversized pullover.

Google how to sew in shoulder pads and – surprise, surprise – you will find a thousand and one ways of doing it correctly. But I just took a needle and thread and sewed mine in. A few stitches in normal sewing cotton on the narrow edges plus a couple more on the longer edges and you're done. After all, they don't have to last forever, for goodness sake! And luckily, we have the right of revocation: if they go out of fashion again after five minutes, you can take them out whenever you want.

Shoulder pads are available to buy in various sizes, depending on how much fill you want. In my experience, original 1980s shoulder pads are best. If you have any tucked away anywhere or kicking around, then dig them out. Or maybe use shoulder pads from an old jacket? Other than that, there's just my usual piece of advice: check the recycling. But be quick, because now that they're back in fashion, they'll be going like hot cakes. You can also get shoulder pads in any fabric or textile shop, but make sure they are good quality because that way, you can hang on to them, ready for when they come back into fashion in 25 years' time.

Instructions

Let It All Hang Out Scarf

Basic yarn ★ Depends on what size of needle you have chosen, but black, white, grey, brown and beige are always good to give the eye a break. For my scarf I used e.g. 1 strand Peruvian Highland Wool plus 1 strand Tilia, to suit needle size 6.

Scrap yarn ★ Varying lengths of thick, thin, smooth and shaggy yarns etc., wound into different sizes of balls and skeins (p. 234). Use 1, 2, 3 or more strands simultaneously. Have a look in your yarn basket or scrap box. Leave your common sense at home. We don't need that here.

Size ★ One size, i.e. width and length as desired.

Total length ★ Scarves come in all lengths. I think a good length is somewhere between 160 and 180 cm. But you can also knit a cute, narrow, slightly shorter scarf - like people wore in the 90s.

Yarn requirement ★ You're the boss.

Needles ★ I'd like you to use your favourite needle size, so I can't tell you which size to use. This scarf is all about what's inside you – and knitting it out. There will be highs and lows, so use a needle size you are comfortable with. Whether that's size 3 or 10 – no matter. But of course, your yarn and materials need to fit the needles. So don't forget to take that into account when choosing what size to knit with. You might have a bunch of yarns lying around for needle size 4? I used a size 6, FYI.

Tension square ★ Irrelevant on this project. Just go for it!

Whaaat? No recommended needle size? Surely not! Well, believe me when I say: there is no recommended needle size for this scarf. And no recommended tension either. And in a moment, you'll notice there are no real knitting instructions for it either. Because it doesn't matter. None needed. And this project is totally yours. This scarf is all about knitting out whatever is inside you and wants to see the light of day: memories, inspirations, thoughts, obsessions, ideas, colours and techniques. Basically, let rip! Open the floodgates! Knit it out!

I knitted the scarf just as I wanted, based on my very own story and on the patterns, colours and materials in this book that seemed to me to fit. I knitted it from within, as it were. And that's what you should do too: knit it from within – in your colours, your techniques and with your patterns and ideas. One thing is for sure: there's more than enough to go round, so let's share, inspire and help each other. If you dare, you could even make a sweater like this. I didn't quite have the guts. Not yet, at least. I haven't got the guts for everything, even though it might look like I have, sometimes.

This scarf is equally beautiful – or ugly – front and back. A bit like life really. Because there is no front and back. I haven't quite finished my scarf yet because I'm a bit of a work in progress myself. So are you. And so is your scarf. Life is a work in progress. Luckily, I still don't know where my scarf is taking me. Not really. And that's why it feels wrong to finish it and cast off. I'll do that at some point, but first I have to live, knit, laugh and cry some more.

>

Let rip! Open the floodgates! Knit it out!

I've never quite had the guts to knit a pullover like this, but maybe sometime soon. If you do, you can use the pattern for the *Fancy Sweater* (p. 132) as your basis, but without the houndstooth.

This scarf is a mix and remix of everything in this book that seemed to me to fit.

There is no front or back. Both sides look equally good. Just put bits of front and back on both sides.

CHANEL

Basic instructions

Casting on ★ Cast on an odd number of sts. It has to be odd so that the ribbing at the end looks good. PS: I cast on 67 sts. BUTT, then twisted rib (k1 tbl, p1), k1 at end. Work ribbing to desired length, e.g. 5-10 cm. The wider and longer the scarf, the better a longer section of ribbing will look. So, if you can, knit quite a lot of ribbing. I struggle to get the right balance myself, and everything within me just screams, "Can't be bothered! Boring!". And that's why my ribbing is always 3 cm shorter than intended.

Edges ★ Now for my second-most important tip on knitting a nice scarf: the edges. Very important. You'll be switching between god knows how many techniques, patterns and materials, so an element of consistency is important. And that element is the edges. So, on either side of the scarf, work 5-10 sts in ribbing so that your edges don't roll in. *Technically, that means knitting* › BUTT, k1 tbl, p1, k1 tbl, p1 and so on until 5 sts remain. p1 tbl, k1 tbl, p1 tbl, k1 tbl, k1. Turn and rep. Make the edge wider than 5 sts if you wish. And from now on, just use whatever techniques, patterns and colours you like. I have a few tips on those as well, of course. You are probably asking yourself: what's the most important tip for knitting this scarf? Let me tell you: relax and enjoy it. And remember: It doesn't have to look beautiful. As long as the chaos has a little touch of beauty to it somewhere.

Casting off ★ When you think your scarf is long enough, finish with the same ribbing as you did at the start. Cast off. Congratulations! Great job!

Dos and Don'ts for the *Let It All Hang Out Scarf*

- ★ Every time you change pattern, you could knit a few rows of stocking stitch to give the next pattern space to breathe.
- ★ This scarf doesn't have a front and back, so knit a bit in stocking stitch and a bit in reverse stocking stitch to give it a bit of oomph.
- ★ The edges of this scarf will be wonky. There's no way of avoiding that. Just accept it and enjoy it. The longer a patterned section, the more the edge will bulge in or out. If you want to keep the bulges a bit more even, knit no more than about 3-4 cm for each section.
- ★ **As for the edges:** › IMPORTANT – knit the borders on either side in twisted rib all the way up the entire scarf. I forgot on various occasions and had to un-knit what I had done. A twisted rib border more or less holds the whole thing together. If you are knitting a pattern in multiple colours, I think it looks best if you choose just one of them as your edge colour (see photos on p. 220-221).
- ★ When you cut off your yarn, leave an end of 10-15 cm. Just leave it hanging. You can always knot it in later. Either leave it dangling or sew it in and cut it off.
- ★ You will probably need to add or subtract a few stitches as you go, to accommodate your colour design. Likely just a stitch or two. It doesn't do any harm to increase or decrease a stitch to get the number specified on your colour chart. All a bit controversial, I know, but hey, this is your scarf, so you do what you like with it. Knit the increase or decrease in the middle. That way it will be nigh-on – or even totally – impossible to see. After all, out of sight, out of mind...
- ★ If you need a break from all your ideas and insights, just switch to a colour or yarn you find calming. You could even knit a cute little row of holes, as shown on p. 43.
- ★ Maybe you have a particularly amazing stash of precious materials you can't bear to part with? Well, perhaps this is the time? It could be a really special yarn of your grandma's, or a load of musk ox yarn your dad bought you in Greenland just before he died.

cute

Guide

Den Norske Genser (the Norwegian pullover)

I'd like to finish this book with a really beautiful knit. And what could be more suitable than my interpretation of a Norwegian leisure-nature-couture sweater that my dad would probably have thought silly but still loved anyway. In terms of function, it doesn't really tick all the boxes. But in terms of being too crazy, it certainly does! And that's what really matters!

In 2022 I was in Norway for a TV shoot and was tasked with producing a homage to the traditional Norwegian pullover, the *Norske Genser*, in just four days. The result was really funky, though I say it myself. In fact, this is one of the best designs I've ever made. There were a lot of requests for the instructions. A LOT. But to be honest, this sweater is so impossible that I can't actually write proper instructions for it. Instead, I developed a guide. And from hereon in, knit at your own risk! But then, you know that already, right...?

First of all, choose a yarn that suits the needle size you want to use. (Don't choose cotton or bamboo, they are too hard.) You can use anything from size 3 to size 8 mm needles – it's completely up to you. Knit a swatch to work out your tension. The front and back of the sweater will be slightly narrower than your actual chest measurement.

So, how do you work out how my stitches you need? Let me explain using my own measurements. I used Fritidsgarn and size 8 needles (p. 254) to get approx. 12 stitches for 10 cm (= 1.2 stitches per cm). My chest measurement is approx. 84 cm. So, to work out how many stitches you need, multiply your chest measurement by your tension (number of stitches) per cm. In my case that's:

84 cm × 1.2 sts per cm = 100.8 sts

Now subtract a bit because this sweater needs to be a snug fit. It mustn't be baggy. For myself, I would probably cast on between 88 and 96 stitches, depending on the pattern. And now you have to choose your pattern as well.

But REMEMBER › You can knit with size 4 needles if you like but need to adapt the numbers accordingly.

Choose a pattern. Any pattern. Your favourite pattern: houndstooth, Norwegian star motifs, flowers, louse patterns, statements – whatever. You can also knit the *genser* without a pattern and use sequins, beads or nothing at all. If you knit a pattern, you will need to adapt the number of stitches to accommodate it, preferably using border stitches (p. 207) to help you get the number pattern stitches you need.

Now start knitting the bodice. Cast on X number of stitches and knit ribbing in rows until you have the desired length. Don't forget the BUTTs. When it's time, switch to stocking stitch or your chosen pattern. Knit the desired length – whether crop top or pullover – then cast off all sts and cut off yarn.

Now for the sleeves. Measure around your arms at their widest point and work out the number of stitches you need like you did with your chest measurement. With the sleeves, you don't need to subtract anything because you want to be able to pull them up comfortably over your shoulders. When you know how many stitches you need at the top of your sleeve, add another 20 – because as we work our way up, we are going to dec ten times (on both sides).

30 cm × 1.2 sts per cm = 36 sts (around the upper arm)

36 stitches + 20 stitches = 56 stitches (at the wrist)

Adapt the number of stitches for your sleeve to suit your pattern, like you did with the bodice. Now cast on X number of stitches again and knit in stocking stitch. BUTT the edges on both sides, and dec 1 after every 2.5 cm.

>

Genius! Great job! Well done, me! Praise where praise is due – for yourself and other people.

Truly awesome online style.

Rep 10 times, until you have the number of stitches you calculated for your upper arm.

When the sleeve is the right length, cast off. Try it on in front of the mirror. If it looks good, knit the second sleeve the same way.

Cool! So, let's get ready to assemble it and finish off the edges. I used a contrast colour, but it's up to you what you use. With a crochet hook that's the same size as your needles, crochet the sleeve seams together in double crochets, with RS facing you. Now do a round of double crochets all around the top and bottom edges.

Crochet all around the bodice too, in double crochet. Start at the bottom edge of the left front and work your way up the front edge, round the top and back, and then all the way down the right front. On every corner, do three double crochets into the same stitch to create a nice, rounded edge. When you're done, cut off the yarn.

Now crochet the sleeves onto the bodice. This is going to look so great! Again, start at the bottom of the left front and do double crochets, just as before, until you get to the point where the armhole would be. Crochet one sleeve on and continue across the top of it to the back of the bodice. Then work your way across to the other armhole and attach the second sleeve. Finish at the bottom of the right front.

If needed, you can link the sleeves across the back with a crocheted band consisting of 2 rows of double crochets. Knit or sew the band onto the edge of the sleeves.

Sew in, knot or do whatever with any loose ends, then sew on hooks to close the front. (I bought my hooks at Sandnes Garn, but they are available from lots of different Norwegian online shops.)

Great things polarise people. They always have. And great emotions are good, whether admiration or the opposite. It's the same with this *genser*. Trust me.

LANG
BREEZE
PINEAPPLE

Greatest Hits

by Lærke Bagger

For *Norsk Genser* guide, see p. 224.

Yarn types › The four I use most

Wool ★ A stretchy yarn that's good for beginners. The fibres pull together nicely when you have finished, making the stitches more even than something like cotton.

Cotton ★ Good for more experienced knitters. It takes a little more skill to get the stitches nice and even, as cotton does not stretch. It falls beautifully and naturally but is not ideal for larger, heavier pullovers.

Mohair ★ Leaves fluff everywhere, all over your clothes, but is great to work with. And because it's so light and fine, it is perfect for blending with another yarn in double-stranded knitting. It is also great for ombre knitting, i.e. creating a colour gradient.

Novelty (special-effect) yarns ★ Acrylic, faux-fur and nylon yarns are novelty yarns – basically anything that adds a special effect to your project. You may be able to find these types of yarns in your local second-hand shop (p. 212).

Basic yarns › Yarns for a little peace and quiet

Your basic yarn is the leitmotif of your garment, the basic colour of the project. Amid all the crazy, in-your-face shades, your basic yarn is an oasis of calm. It helps bring your knitting together visually, tames it and adds harmony. With Fair Isle knitting, there's basic yarn 1 and basic yarn 2, one being the main colour, the other being the pattern colour – because Fair Isle is about knitting with two colours, of course.

Scrap yarn › The essence of knitting with Lærke Bagger

Scrap yarn comprises remnants of anything and everything: cut-off ends, annoying leftover balls of wool, bad purchases, individual balls bought on impulse and yarns you have picked up at second-hand shops. It's time to knit the stuff you thought was too frumpy to knit. There are all sorts of ways you can use it – three of which I demonstrated as scrap techniques in my first book. You can use them to make the garments in this book as well. The three scrap techniques are:

ATS (Alone Together Sweater technique) ★ Cut off your basic yarn from time to time and knit with a strand of scrap instead. When you have knitted in a section in scrap, knot your basic yarn back on and carry on knitting with that. The result will be a mix of scrap and basic yarns throughout your garment.

All-Over ★ This involves knitting an entire garment from self-made yarns that you have created from scraps. To create your yarn, knot different lengths of scrap yarn together end to end and wind them into balls. You can either wind entire balls or just make smaller skeins. If you are going to knit double-stranded and blend your All-Over scraps with a basic yarn, it looks good if you wind your basic yarn around your scraps. If you combine scrap yarn with your pattern colour in a Fair Isle project, it will give you All-Over Fair Isle patterns.

Bad Idea ★ This technique is all about knitting stripes with different lengths of leftover yarns. For your basic yarns, choose subdued colours. Combine with colourful special-effect yarns so that they complement each other (or not, if you prefer). Knit a bit, cut off the thread, change colour, knot it in, stop, go back a bit, carry on again.

Colour compositions › How to

These tips and techniques will help you develop the perfect colour combination.

Have no fear ★ If you worry too much, it will stop you from doing things. So, be brave! Use colours that clash, for instance. It shows you have attitude.

See colours in context ★ How do your colours speak to each other? Do they scream at each other like red and yellow or whisper to each other like pale blue and white? It's up to you to decide how they should communicate with each other.

Coordinate your colours ★ Colour composition matters. Do you want to use different shades of the same colour? Don't forget some subdued colours for a break in between. Coordinate the colours to express what you want.

Work with contrasts ★ Contrast doesn't necessarily mean a colour contrast, like yellow and blue; cool and warm shades of the same colour are a contrast too.

Try out your ideas ★ Don't just go with your first idea. Your next one could be just as good. And your third one could be even better! Challenge yourself a bit!

Analysis is your friend ★ Think about what you want your knitting project to achieve. Ask yourself how you are going to attain your goals.

Windings ★ Cut out some smallish rectangles of cardboard and wind the yarns you are thinking of combining around them. Tape the strands to the back of the card. You can now see how the yarns look together.

Visualise ★ Make windings or sketch colour gradients to help you visualise the finished product in different colour combinations.

Lay it all out ★ Spread out lots of different-coloured yarns on the table or floor. Choose a few, put different colours side by side, remove any shades you don't think fit, play around and mix and match as the mood takes you. Follow your intuition!

Be flexible in your search ★ Take a piece of white A4 or A3 card and cut a square out of the middle with a craft knife. Lay the square over all sorts of things: your favourite painting, a photo, a book. Use the finder in all sorts of different places, look at the colours and then choose those colours of yarn.

Fancy Bag (p. 126).

Tips and tricks for colour knitting (Fair Isle, p. 80)

Changing colour › **It's easy!**

To switch colour, simply knot the new colour in and carry on knitting. If you are changing colours for a Fair Isle motif and need to switch on a particular stitch, there is a special way of doing it (p. 74).

The knot that never comes undone › **Just tie knots!**

a Lay the two ends you want to knot so they are parallel.

b Tie a normal knot – which I call a parallel knot.

c Lay the two ends across each other and knot them crosswise.

d Place the ends side by side again and tie another parallel knot.

e Give the ends a good tug and cut them off 2-3 mm from the knot.

3-Day Sweater (p. 54). *Barbie 3-Day Sweater* (p. 60). Sequins (p. 210).

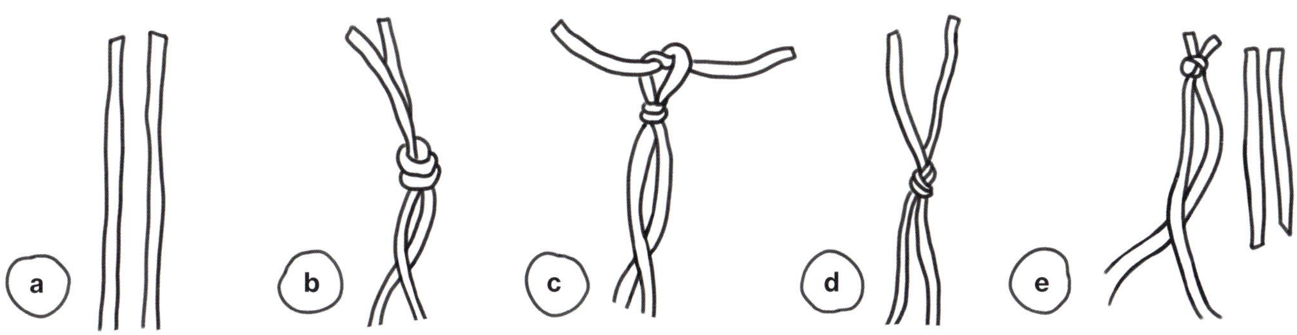

Ombre effect on a *Fancy Bag* (p. 126).

Fancy Bag (p. 126) and *Family Sweater (for grownups*, p. 86).

Fancy Sweater (p. 132).

Tension › **Mandatory stuff**

You can find out your tension by doing a tension square. This is a 10 x 10 cm square that's knitted in the recommended yarn with the recommended needle size and in the pattern described in your instructions.

Counting the number of stitches across 10 cm of your knitting gives you your stitch gauge – which could be something like 11 stitches. Counting the number of rows tells you your row gauge – 13 rows, for example. So your tension is 11 stitches and 13 rows for 10 x 10 cm.

Some of the items in this book are made with different types of yarn. Where this is the case, you can use the different yarns for your tension square and, if need be, knit a bigger one. Then count the stitches and rows in various places and work out the average. All the instructions in this book are based on my own tension, by the way, not that of the yarn producer or yourself. The point of a tension square is to find out your own tension.

If your tension square gives you a different number of stitches than the number you need, change needles. If you have too many stitches making up 10 cm, try thicker needles. If you have too few stitches making up 10 cm, try thinner ones. But don't let your tension square control you. This is supposed to be fun!

Size guide › **Love yourself**

I want to get away from traditional sizes like XS and XXXL because I find them discriminatory and misleading. They are based on standard measurements that are actually not standard at all. My advice is: measure yourself and use the numbers to help you estimate what size to knit. Every set of instructions tells you where exactly you need to measure.

But to be able to give you fair guidance, I need to categorise each size. So instead of XS, S, M, L, XL, XXL, XXXL and XXXXL, I call my sizes 1, 2, 3, 4, 5, 6, 7 and 8 because to me, that just makes the most sense.

Negative/positive ease › **Space to move**

The "ease" of a garment is the difference between the wearer's body measurements and the dimensions of the item itself.

Positive ease is when the dimensions of the garment are larger than your body measurements. As a rule of thumb, positive ease tends to be between 5 and 10 cm. That means you need to choose the size that is 5-10 cm larger than your body. So, if your chest measurement is 98 cm, choose a garment size with a chest measurement of between 103 and 108 cm. If you want extra width, choose a size that will give you more ease.

Negative ease means the garment is smaller than your body, e.g. *the 3-Day Sweater/Dress/Top/Skirt* (p. 54). This has a lot of negative ease because it needs to be a snug fit on your body. When you put it on, it will stretch a lot.

Wrong-side row › **A great tip**

If you are doing stocking stitch, always knit the purls on your wrong-side rows on a smaller needle than specified in the instructions. That will give you a nice, even finish. Do this not only on projects knitted in rows but also on ones where the front and back are knitted in the rounds and the neck section is knitted in rows. So, for your wrong-side rows, use a needle that's a size smaller. If you are knitting with a circular needle that has interchangeable points, it's easy.

Magic Loop › **For those who hate double-pointed needles**

★ Pull all your stitches onto the cable of your circular needle. Distribute them evenly and pull the section of cable out that's between the middle stitches.

★ Push the front stitches onto your left needle and knit as required.

★ Distribute the stitches evenly again, push them onto the left needle and knit.

★ Continue as described.

If it's gotta be,
it's gotta be.

The BUTT › Queen of edge stitches

1 On the first stitch in the row, pull the working thread in front of the needle back and up to create what looks like a double stitch.

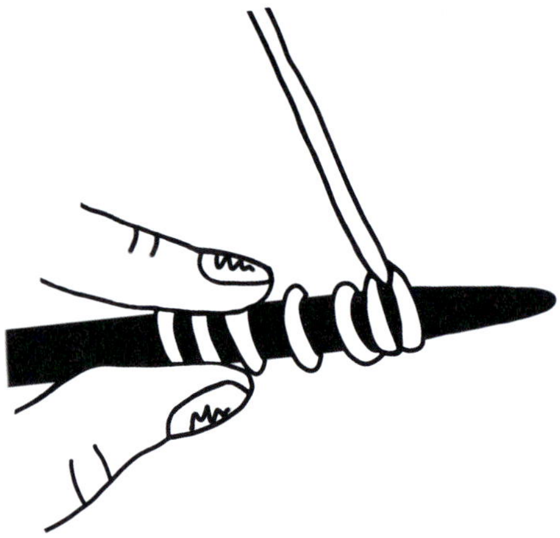

2 Work this stitch by inserting your right needle into it from the back and slipping it off the needle – without actually knitting it.

3 ALWAYS work the last stitch of every row in knit on both wrong as well as right-side rows.

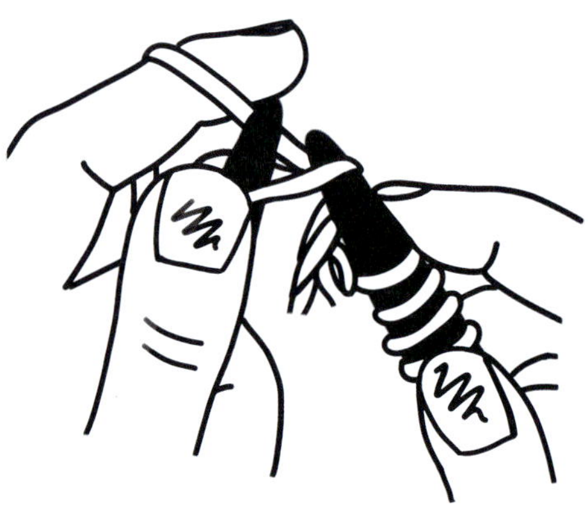

Knit from bottom to top › For the nicest neckline

My garments are all knitted from bottom to top because that way, I find it easier to get the proportions of the neckline right. After all, the neckline is one of the nicest things on a sweater! If you have not quite managed to keep your tension right and notice your neckline is going to be too tight or too deep, it will be easier to fix if you are knitting from bottom to top. Simply cast off fewer or more stitches than specified and you will end up with a neckline that fits you perfectly.

The sleeves are knitted from bottom to top too. Try them on from time to time and knit them longer or shorter so they fit. Do the same with the front and back. Adapt the length by making them longer or shorter before you get to the armhole.

Necklines › The eye-catching feature of a sweater

A beautiful neckline in two steps.

1 Always pick up stitches for your neckline with the right side of your work facing you and in knit stitch. Start in the middle of the back. Pick up 9 stitches across every ten rows. In other words, skip every tenth row, unless specified otherwise. Pick up your stitches through just one of the two loops of each edge stitch – otherwise the seam will be too bulky. If the garment is very light, thin or fine, use the inner loop. With thicker garments use the outer one.

2 Knit the neck ribbing as long or short as you want. If you want the edge to be flat, cast off in rib stitch.

Twisted rib › The graphic statement
Whether rollneck, sleeve, neckline or edge – twisted rib always looks great.

k1 tbl, p1, repeat to end.

Armholes › When you're nearly done!

1 With your work inside out, lay the cast-off armhole edge on the front and back against the cast-off edge of the sleeve.

2 Crochet the two pieces together using slip stitch (p. 244). Push your hook from right to left through the outer loops of the stitches on the pieces.

3 Repeat on other sleeve.

Let It All Hang Out Scarf (p. 218).

Inner Child Sweater (p. 48).

Family Sweater (p. 86) and *Family Beanie* (p. 96).

Nah, not the cheese ones, the spicy chicken ones!

Raglan › **With right- and left-leaning decreases**

Raglan seams run from the bottom of the armhole up across the collarbone to the neckline. A raglan pullover has four raglan seams: two at the front and two at the back. They are formed by decreasing as you knit from bottom to top – which is the chosen method for all of the instructions in this book.

Two ways of knitting decreases

Right-leaning decrease › Knit 2 together (k2tog)

Left-leaning decrease › Slip 1, knit 1, pass slipped stitch over the knitted stitch (SKP)

Increasing › **Two options**

Inc 1 › Pick up the horizontal thread between two stitches (from the front, using your left needle), then knit the stitch through back of loop (tbl)

Alternatively:

Inc 1 › k1 or p1 but leave the stitch on needle, then k1 or p1 into the same stitch through back of loop and slide off the needle. For a knit stitch, this is called kfb (knit through front and back), for a purl it is call pfb (purl through front and back). This method is particularly good for increases on the base of the *Fancy Bag* (p. 126).

You may need to increase x number of stitches evenly across a piece. This means increasing x number of times using the above technique, with a similar number of stitches between each increase.

Casting on additional stitches at the end of a row › **Here's how!**

e.g. for a thumb hole on the *Inner Child Sweater* (p. 48).

1 Hold the needle that needs the extra stitches in your right hand. Loop the yarn around your left thumb.

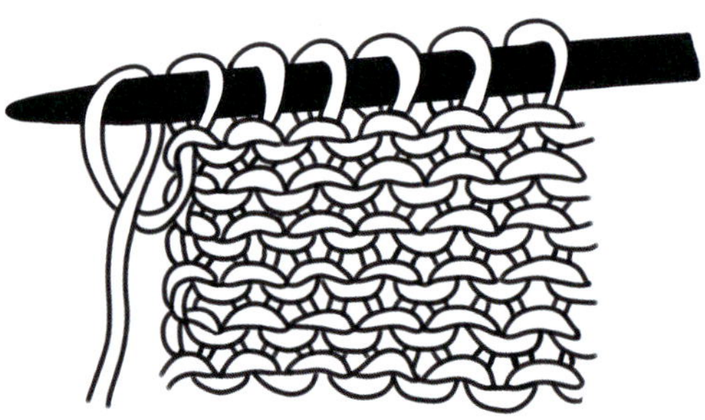

2 Push the point of the needle up through the loop on your left thumb and pull your thumb out. Give the new stitch a nice tug so it sits firmly on the needle.

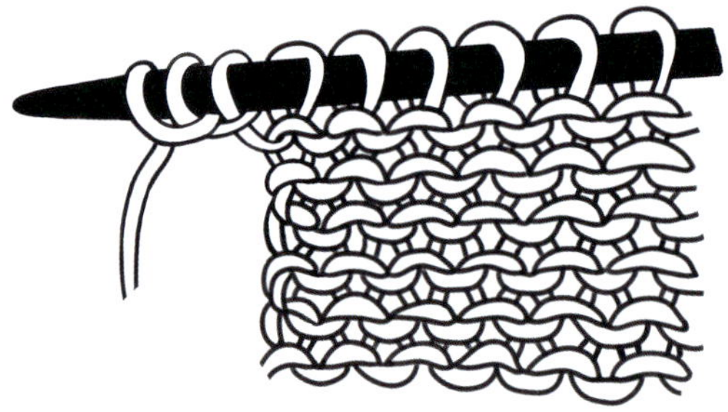

3 Repeat until you have added the desired number of stitches.

Crochet stitches › The two types I use most

Slip stitch (ss)

Push the crochet hook into the stitch, yarn over, then pull the thread through both loops on the hook.

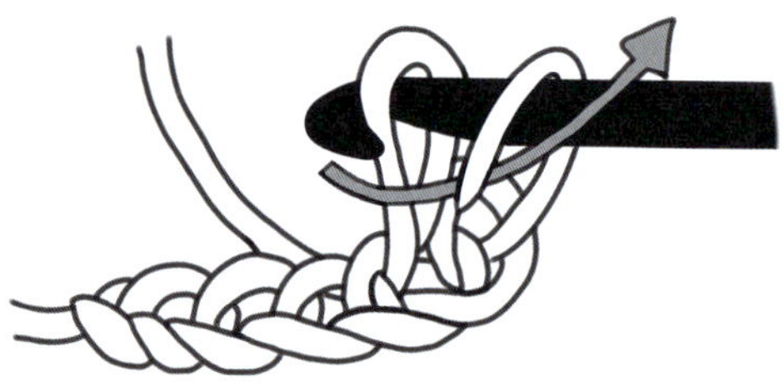

Single crochet (sc)

1 Push the crochet hook into the stitch, yarn over, then pull the thread back through the stitch. You now have two loops on your hook.

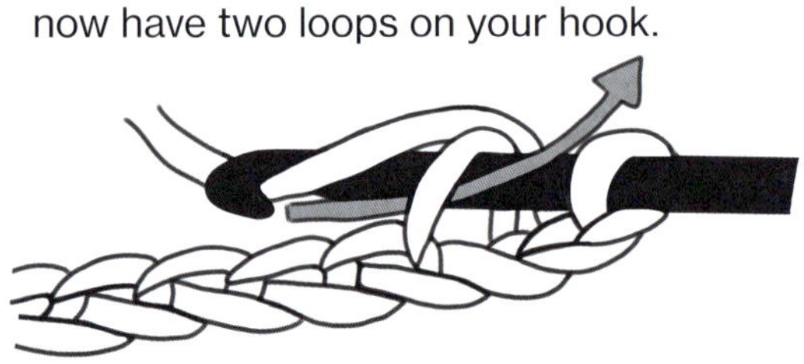

2 Yarn over and pull the thread through both loops on the hook.

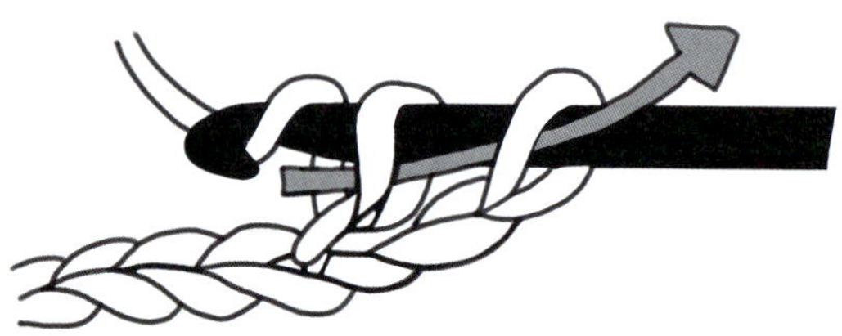

Inner Child Sweater
(p. 48).

Assembling pieces › **The magic of slip stitch**

To assemble pieces with slip stitch like this, you will need a neat knitted edge – with BUTT stitches, for example (p. 242). You can use slip stitch for anything: closing side, sleeve and shoulder seams, fixing fold-down necks, closing up armholes and attaching pockets, ribbing and so on.

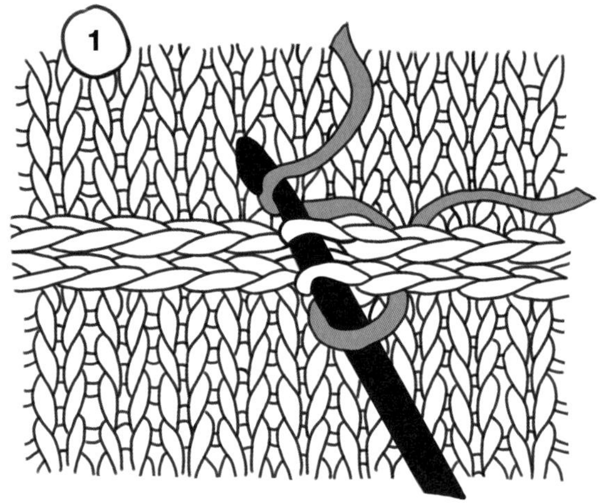

Before you start, here's a tip: unless specified otherwise, always work with the right side of your work facing you. Push the hook through just one of the two loops in each edge stitch. That way the seam won't turn out so bulky. But only if not stated otherwise.

Assembling pieces with slip stitch

Lay the two pieces you want to join next to each other, edge to edge. Work from right to left. Decide whether you want to use the inner or outer loop of the edge stitch – and stick with it.

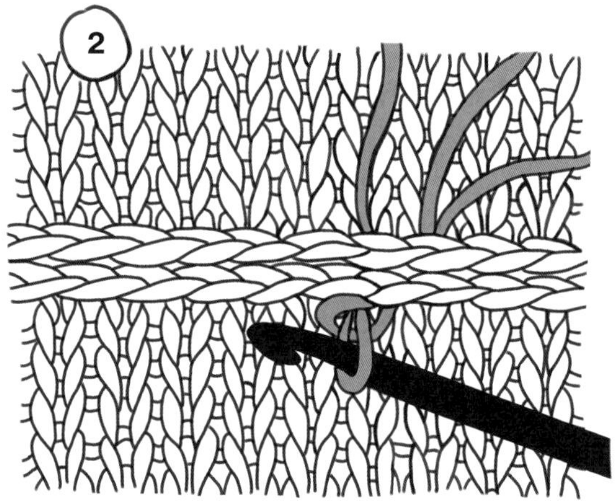

1 Push the crochet hook through, say, the outer loop of one edge stitch and the outer loop of its counterpart on the second knitted piece. Yarn over, and then pull the strand through both of the loops.

2 Repeat with the outer loops of the next pair of edge stitches. You now have two loops on your hook. Next, without a yarn over, pull the new loop through the first loop. This will leave you with just one stitch on your hook again. You have now crocheted two edge stitches into a seam while "casting off" one stitch.

3 Push the hook through the loop of the next knitted edge stitch and continue as described until you have joined the two pieces together all the way along.

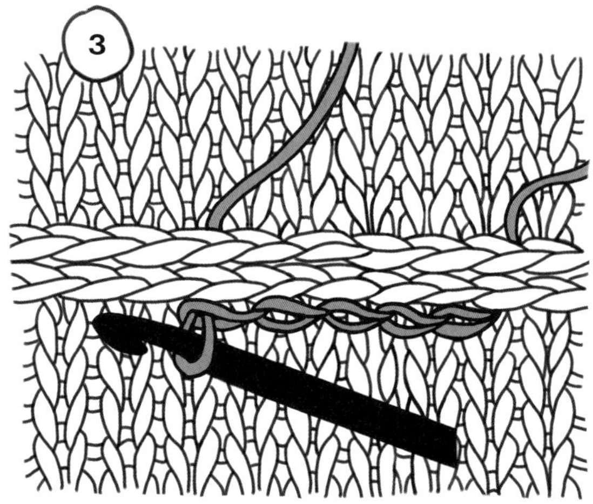

Very important technique.

Family Sweater, for grownups (p. 86) and kids (p. 92).

Inner Child Sweater (p. 48).

Fancy Tube Top (p. 142).

Treatment and care › If absolutely necessary

I rarely treat my knits in any way because I find it makes the stitches look flat and lifeless. But you might think differently, of course. And there are indeed some garments in this book where the end result does look much better if you give them a bit of an iron.

Those garments are: the *Fancy Cardy/Sweater* (p. 132), the *Fancy Tube Top* (p. 142) and the *Family Sweater* (for grownups p. 86 and kids p. 92).

How to press your knit

★ Spray a towel with a little water to dampen it, then sandwich your knit into it. Towel, knit, towel. Put some books on top and leave to lie for a half or whole day.

★ Use a pressing cloth – If you are going to use an iron, use a damp tea or hand towel and mind you don't press down too hard.

If you really want to, you can treat your knits

★ Steam them with a steamer or iron. This may flatten the fibres.

★ Air if necessary after multiple wears.

★ Wash only if really necessary. Use cold water and handwash with a suitable detergent, e.g. wool detergent for knits. Dry flat between two towels. For kids' knits, use the washing machine and a wool programme.

Yarn requirements › Estimating amounts

I have spent a lot of time on all sorts of things I think I should be able to do but am actually totally useless at. These include baking cakes, packing suitcases and writing knitting instructions with definitive yarn quantities.

I am SO good at all sorts of other things, like the Italian lyrics to Eros Ramazotti's *Più Bella Cosa*, paying for rounds in the pub, and inspiring people to knit without rules and just enjoy it.

But I have come to the point where I just don't want to waste any more time on things I'm useless at. And quite frankly, it's nigh-on impossible to give exact figures on required yarn quantities anyway because I like instructions that allow you to vary the knit by using myriad types of yarn. So, yarn quantities here are only ever vague estimates. But fear not – it's the perfect excuse for growing your stash.

My advice on yarn requirements

Always buy too much rather than too little. They'll come in handy at some point, I promise you!

With my designs, it doesn't really matter if all the balls are from the same dye lot, as they will be mixed, blended and felted with other yarns and patterns.

Carpe diem! And don't worry, be happy!

A word on length › Don't hate the player – hate the game!

Unfortunately, I can't tell you exactly how long to knit the garments in this book. Just knit them so they fit you. They can all be knitted short or long. So, measure your body and take a good look at yourself. Hold your work up to yourself from time to time, look in the mirror and decide what to do next. Imagine you're at the hairdressers reading gossip mags and you never look up to see what the hairdresser is doing. You could end up with your hair too short. That's pretty risky. So, take a look at your knitting from time to time.

Carpe diem! And don't worry, be happy!

1 Using a needle, thread the right number of beads onto your yarn. If the yarn is too thick for the eye of the needle, thread some sewing cotton through the needle instead, knot the ends together, and then "thread" your yarn through the loop this creates. When you have got enough beads onto your yarn, simply remove the needle.

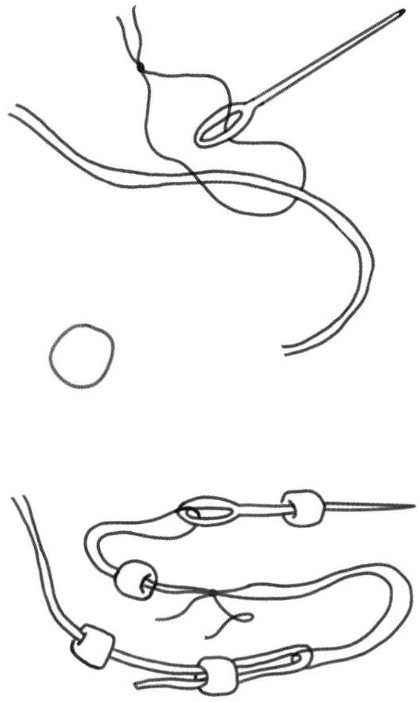

2 As you knit, keep pushing the beads down your yarn to give you enough length to knit with.

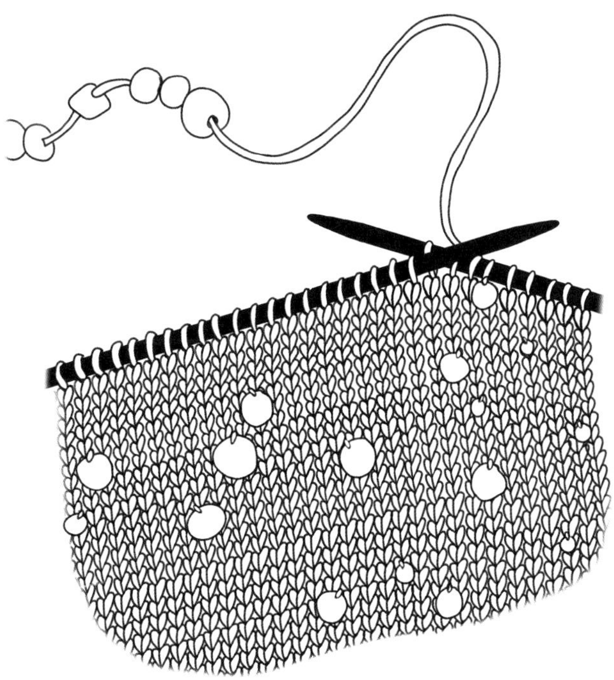

3 When you get to a place where you want to knit in a bead, pull the first bead on your yarn up and knit it in with your next plain stitch. Your bead will now be on the front of your work. Now continue in the same way.

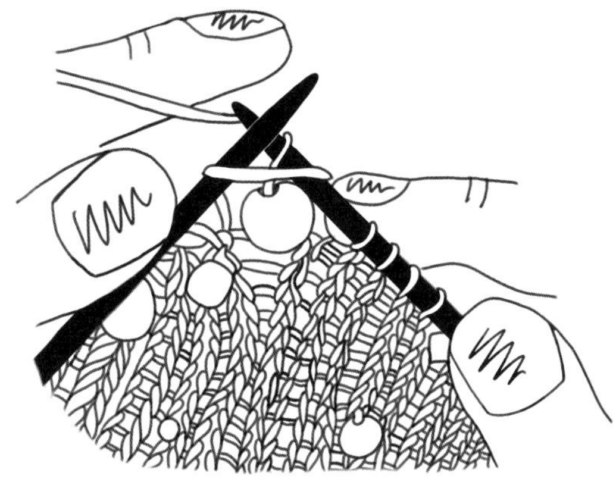

4 On the next row or round, when you get to the stitch with the knitted-in bead, fix it in place by knitting into the back of the loop.

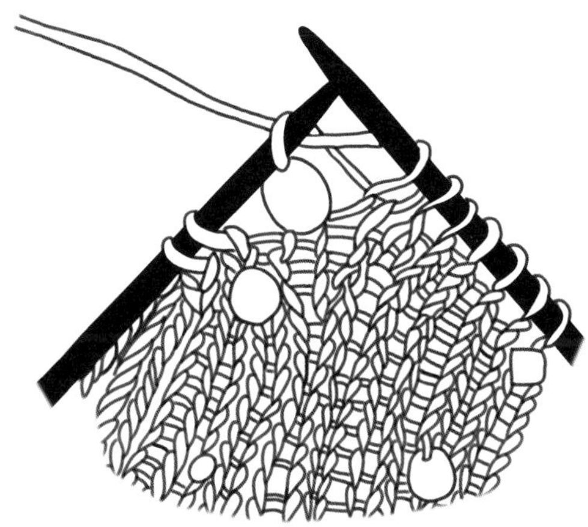

BY 69 771

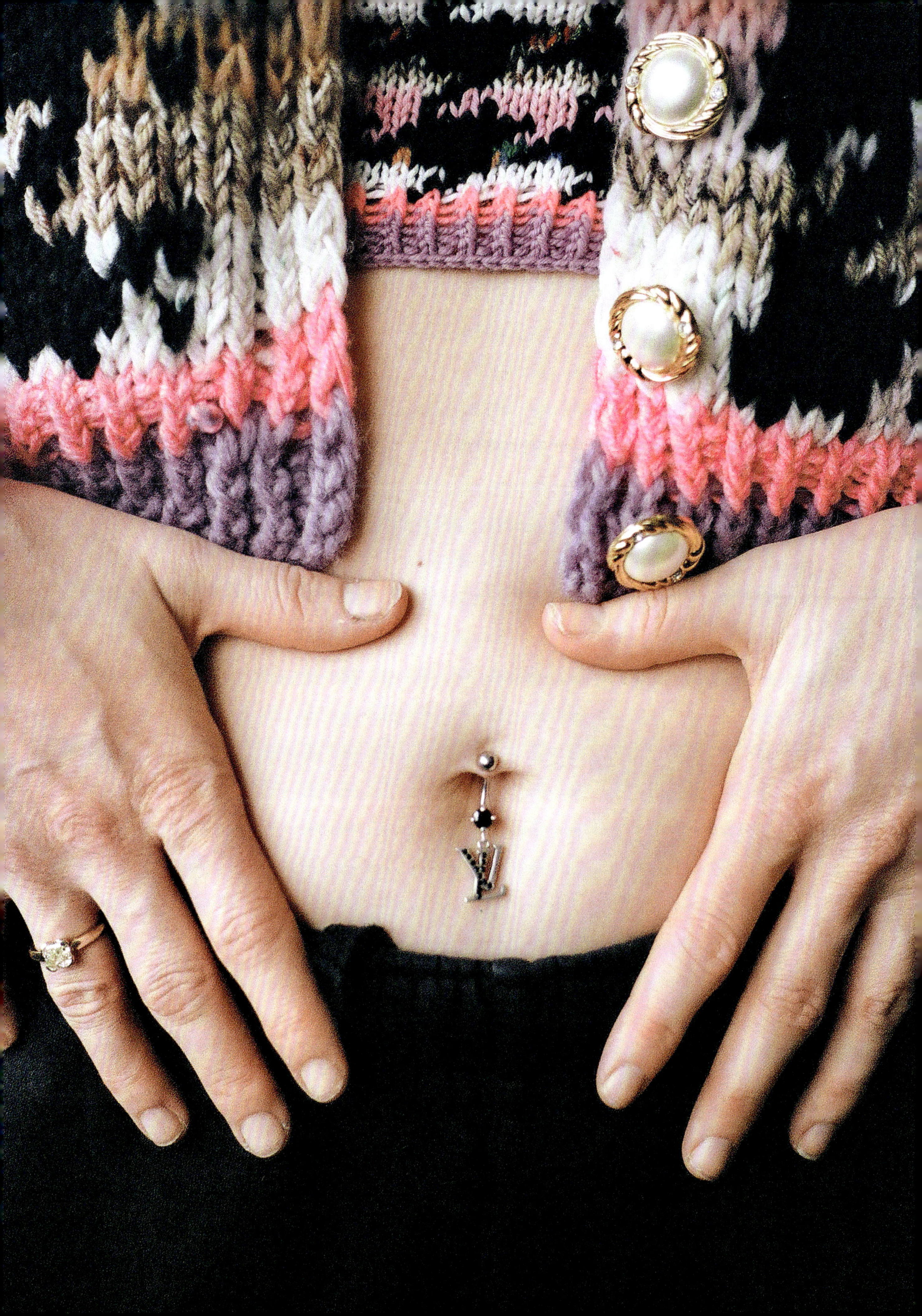

Yarn types

This section lists all the yarns used in this book. They are easy to replace with alternatives. Simply ask your local wool shop about other options. And you might even get a cup of coffee from them! I quite often use different yarn types within a single garment that don't even match in terms of gauge or length, e.g. for entrelac (p. 159) or the Inner Child technique (p. 37). I just can't help myself! But most of the time it does work out.

If you want to use a different yarn from the one specified, I recommend using something where the 50- or 100-gram ball has a similar yardage, gauge and needle size. Most yarn types – wool, cotton, mohair etc. – are available from different manufacturers in similar forms.

Abbreviations ›

dec; decs	decrease, decreases
dpn	double-pointed needle
inc; incs	increase, increases
k	knit (plain)
k2tog	knit 2 together (decrease)
p	purl
pfb	purl through front and back
rnd; rnds	round; rounds
RS	right side
SKP	slip 1, knit 1, pass slipped stitch over
st; sts	stitch/stitches
St st	stocking stitch
tbl	through back of loop
tog	together
WS	wrong side

Filcolana

Peruvian Highland Wool
100% Peruvian highland wool
50 g = approx. 100 m
Tension › approx. 16-20 sts on needle size 4-5 mm

Tilia
70% kid mohair, 30% silk
25 g = 210 m
Tension › Check with your local wool shop

Arwetta
80% superwash merino wool, 20% nylon
50 g = 210 m
Tension › approx. 28-32 sts on needle size 2.5-3 mm

Lang Yarns

Mille Colori Baby
100% merino wool
50 g = 190 m
Tension › approx. 27 sts on needle size 3-3.5 mm

Cloud
90% merino wool, 10% polyamide
100 g = 260 m
Tension › approx. 13 sts on needle size 7 mm

Phoenix
93% merino wool, 7% polyamide
100 g = 270 m
Tension › approx. 9 sts on needle size 7-8 mm

Sandnes Garn

Fritidsgarn
100% wool
50 g = 70 m
Tension › approx. 15 sts on needle size 5.5 mm

Brushed Alpaca
96% brushed alpaca, 4% nylon
50 g = 110 m
Tension › approx. 12-16 sts on needle size 5-7 mm

Let's say goodbye, not farewell…

Testfest in my workshop for test knitters for this book.

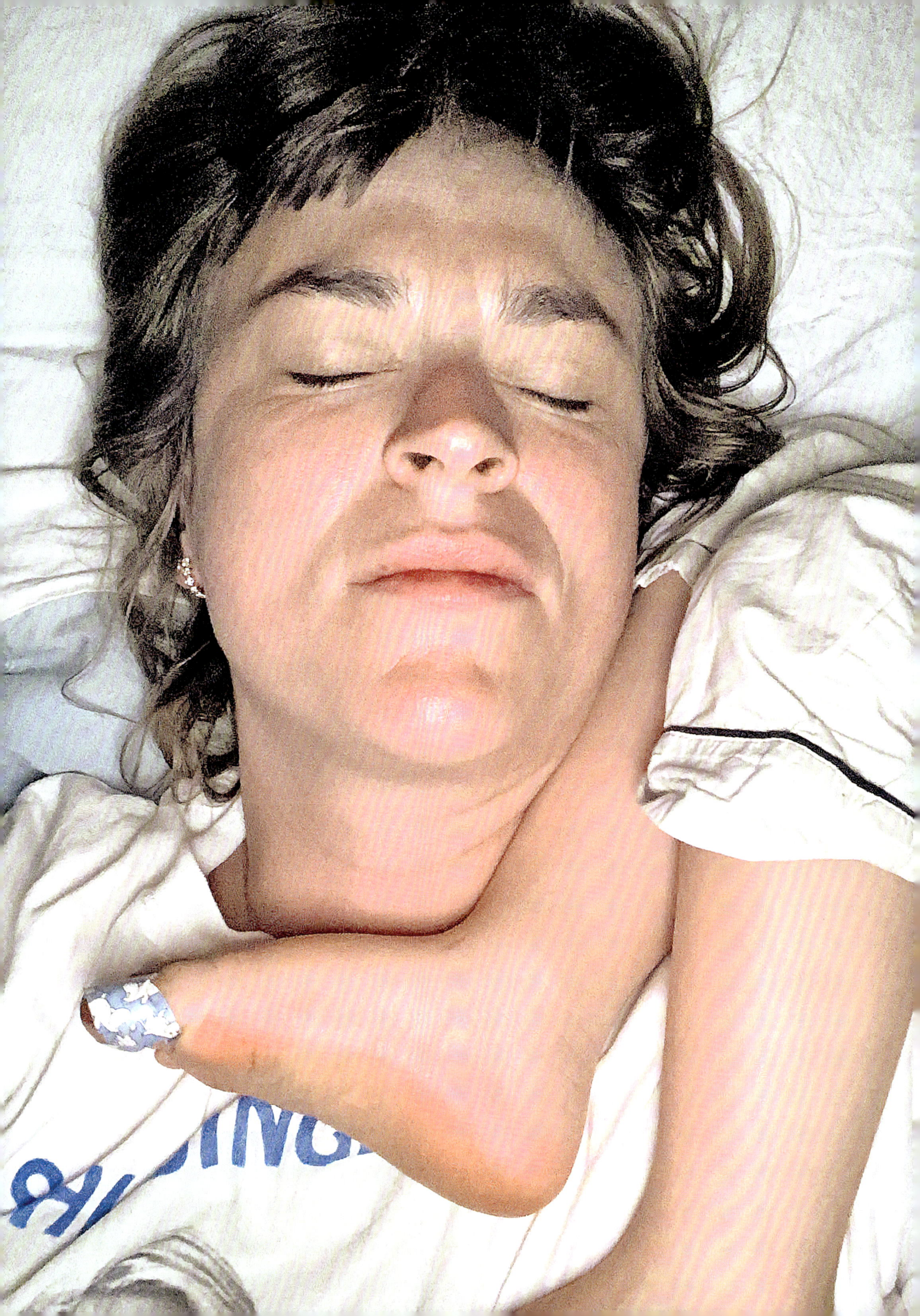

HARV

5 March 2022

Dear Dad,

I think of you every day. At home I have hung the photo of John Lennon next to a picture of you – one where you look cool and are laughing. At your house, you had the John Lennon photo hanging next to a picture of me.

I wrote – and knitted – this book for both of us. For you, but also for me. You will never read it, of course, but to me it feels as though, by writing it, I have come to better understand who you were and who I am, myself.

Between the two of us, we focused on the things that set us apart, on our differences – of which there were many. But we also had a lot in common. We were actually really similar too. But I'm only just seeing that now. And that's what we should have concentrated on.

I often tell Lulu and Lars about grandad Jørn. I want them to know you as a person, to know who you were. They find you really exciting and love hearing about Greenland. These days I find myself telling them all the Greenland stories I found so stupid when I was a kid! Typical, eh? I hope you had a wonderful life in Greenland. It sounded like you did, in your letters. But just imagine I had experienced all that myself!

I think a lot of people will see aspects of themselves in our story. Parents as well as kids. And by telling them about all the stuff we got wrong, maybe I can help them not to waste so much time making exactly the same mistakes as we did.

You were so cool, dammit! I wish I was as cool as you. Nothing is for certain in life, but if there's one thing that is, it's that I'm going back to Greenland. Better late than never. Today I am adding a small, provisional comma to a story that started 38 years ago, when I was born. The comma feels kind of nice. I love you, Dad. Now shut up. We wasted so much precious time, I don't want to waste any more.

Best Laaki

Acknowledgements

I would like to thank Sune, Lulu and Lars. I am so lucky to have you. You are the greatest single thing in my life. Thanks also to Mum and Henning for understanding and supporting my love of Barbie and giving me a good and secure childhood. You're the best parents in the world. And thank you, Anne Marie, for being the sweetest mother-in-law one could ever wish for and always a huge help.

I would also like to thank all my wonderful, hard-working test knitters, who rein me in when things (often) get a bit wild: Frederikke, Mette, Rosa, Sabina, Mikkel, Karla, Benjamin, Mette, Emilie, Sidsel, Siri, Sophie, Anne. And a big thank-you to Anja and Mette and everyone else at Gyldendal who helped make this book possible. Thank you Nethe, Finn, Jacob, Ditte, Sidsel, Christine, Thiemer, Kristoffer, Dal, Ida, Elisabet, Gry and Klara. And last but not least: thank you to Filcolana, Sandnes and Lang Yarns for sponsoring me with fantastic yarns.

I love you all!

51-67
Lærke
Bagger
strik
Lærke Bagger strik

Register

As the wise man sang:

**I guess that now it's time for me to give up
I feel it's time
Got a picture of you beside me
Got your lipstick mark still on your coffee cup
Oh, yeah
Got a fist of pure emotion
Got a head of shattered dreams
Gotta leave it, gotta leave it all behind now**

**Unaware but underlined
I figured out this story (oh, no)
It wasn't good (no, no)
But in the corner of my mind (corner of my mind)
I celebrated glory
But that was not to be
In the twist of separation you excelled at being free
Can't you find a little room inside for me (can't you find, for me)**

G. Barlow, 1997

Listen and enjoy. Let's knit together!

LANG

19.37 5G

21. november 2022
18.35

Rediger

lørdag

Til: info@laerkebagger.com >

Hæklenål

Har lige set jeres udsendelse fra Grønland, og hvor er det sørgeligt at se, at du ikke kan holde rigtigt på en hæklenål. Du ender jo med at få seneskedehindebetændelse, hvis du fortsætter med at hække på den måde. Så for din egen skyld: Få en gammel håndarbejdslærer til at lære dig, hvordan man holder på en hæklenål.

Mvh

Crochet hook: I've just watched a programme about Greenland. It's really sad to see that you don't know how to hold a crochet hook right. If you carry on like that, you'll do yourself an injury. So, for your own benefit, find an old arts and crafts teacher who can show you how it's done. Enjoy!

The end

babygirl